T0384914

An Analysis of

David Hume's

An Enquiry Concerning Human Understanding

Michael O'Sullivan

Published by Macat International Ltd
24:13 Coda Centre, 189 Munster Road, London SW6 6AW.

Dristributed exclusively by Routledge
2 Park Square, Milton Park, Abingdon, Oxon OX14 4RN
711 Third Avenue, New York, NY 10017, USA

Routledge is an imprint of the Taylor & Francis Group, an informa business

www.macat.com
info@macat.com

Cataloguing in Publication Data
A catalogue record for this book is available from the British Library.
Library of Congress Cataloguing-in-Publication Data is available upon request.
Cover illustration: Etienne Gilfillan

ISBN 978-1-912303-01-4 (hardback)
ISBN 978-1-912127-64-1 (paperback)
ISBN 978-1-912281-89-3 (e-book)

Notice
The information in this book is designed to orientate readers of the work under analysis,
to elucidate and contextualise its key ideas and themes, and to aid in the development
of critical thinking skills. It is not meant to be used, nor should it be used, as a
substitute for original thinking or in place of original writing or research. References and
notes are provided for informational purposes and their presence does not constitute
endorsement of the information or opinions therein. This book is presented solely for
educational purposes. It is sold on the understanding that the publisher is not engaged
to provide any scholarly advice. The publisher has made every effort to ensure that
this book is accurate and up-to-date, but makes no warranties or representations with
regard to the completeness or reliability of the information it contains. The information
and the opinions provided herein are not guaranteed or warranted to produce particular
results and may not be suitable for students of every ability. The publisher shall not be
liable for any loss, damage or disruption arising from any errors or omissions, or from
the use of this book, including, but not limited to, special, incidental, consequential or
other damages caused, or alleged to have been caused, directly or indirectly, by the
information contained within.

CONTENTS

THE MACAT LIBRARY

The Macat Library is a series of unique academic explorations of seminal works in the humanities and social sciences – books and papers that have had a significant and widely recognised impact on their disciplines. It has been created to serve as much more than just a summary of what lies between the covers of a great book. It illuminates and explores the influences on, ideas of, and impact of that book. Our goal is to offer a learning resource that encourages critical thinking and fosters a better, deeper understanding of important ideas.

Each publication is divided into three Sections: Influences, Ideas, and Impact. Each Section has four Modules. These explore every important facet of the work, and the responses to it.

This Section-Module structure makes a Macat Library book easy to use, but it has another important feature. Because each Macat book is written to the same format, it is possible (and encouraged!) to cross-reference multiple Macat books along the same lines of inquiry or research. This allows the reader to open up interesting interdisciplinary pathways.

To further aid your reading, lists of glossary terms and people mentioned are included at the end of this book (these are indicated by an asterisk [*] throughout) – as well as a list of works cited.

Macat has worked with the University of Cambridge to identify the elements of critical thinking and understand the ways in which six different skills combine to enable effective thinking.
Three allow us to fully understand a problem; three more give us the tools to solve it. Together, these six skills make up the **PACIER** model of critical thinking. They are:

ANALYSIS – understanding how an argument is built
EVALUATION – exploring the strengths and weaknesses of an argument
INTERPRETATION – understanding issues of meaning

CREATIVE THINKING – coming up with new ideas and fresh connections
PROBLEM-SOLVING – producing strong solutions
REASONING – creating strong arguments

To find out more, visit **WWW.MACAT.COM.**

CRITICAL THINKING AND *AN ENQUIRY CONCERNING HUMAN UNDERSTANDING*

Primary critical thinking skill: ANALYSIS
Secondary critical thinking skill: REASONING

David Hume's 1748 *Enquiry Concerning Human Understanding* is a modern philosophical classic that helped reshape epistemology – the philosophy of knowledge. It is also a classic of the critical thinking skills of analysis and reasoning.

Analysis is all about understanding how arguments work and fit together. Having strong analytical skills helps to break down arguments, pull out the evidence on which they rely, and understand the kinds of implicit assumptions and reasons on which they work. Reasoning, meanwhile, means building and presenting arguments, forming well-structured, evidenced, and organised cases for a particular point of view. Hume applied his analytical skills to arguments about how humans know and understand the world, and how our minds work. At base, he was trying to analyse human reason itself – to show the workings and limitations of the human mind, and show the origins of our beliefs.

Hume went on to apply his reasoning skills, creating an enduring argument about the nature of human knowledge. The result was one of the most striking and famous works in the history of philosophy..

ABOUT THE AUTHOR OF THE ORIGINAL WORK

Born in Edinburgh, Scotland in 1711, the brilliant **David Hume** entered the University of Edinburgh at the age of 12, seemingly destined for a career in academia. But his religious views put him outside the intellectual mainstream. He was skeptical of Christianity and arguably did not believe in God. So Hume became a diplomat and writer, establishing a reputation as one of the finest thinkers of his generation. That reputation has endured: many believe Hume was the greatest philosopher ever to write in English.

ABOUT THE AUTHOR OF THE ANALYSIS

Dr Michael O'Sullivan is a tutor in the Department of Philosophy, King's College London. He is the editor of *Wittgenstein and Perception*.

ABOUT MACAT

GREAT WORKS FOR CRITICAL THINKING

Macat is focused on making the ideas of the world's great thinkers accessible and comprehensible to everybody, everywhere, in ways that promote the development of enhanced critical thinking skills.

It works with leading academics from the world's top universities to produce new analyses that focus on the ideas and the impact of the most influential works ever written across a wide variety of academic disciplines. Each of the works that sit at the heart of its growing library is an enduring example of great thinking. But by setting them in context – and looking at the influences that shaped their authors, as well as the responses they provoked – Macat encourages readers to look at these classics and game-changers with fresh eyes. Readers learn to think, engage and challenge their ideas, rather than simply accepting them.

'Macat offers an amazing first-of-its-kind tool for interdisciplinary learning and research. Its focus on works that transformed their disciplines and its rigorous approach, drawing on the world's leading experts and educational institutions, opens up a world-class education to anyone.'

Andreas Schleicher,
Director for Education and Skills, Organisation for Economic
Co-operation and Development

'Macat is taking on some of the major challenges in university education ... They have drawn together a strong team of active academics who are producing teaching materials that are novel in the breadth of their approach.'

Prof Lord Broers,
former Vice-Chancellor of the University of Cambridge

'The Macat vision is exceptionally exciting. It focuses upon new modes of learning which analyse and explain seminal texts which have profoundly influenced world thinking and so social and economic development. It promotes the kind of critical thinking which is essential for any society and economy. This is the learning of the future.'

Rt Hon Charles Clarke, former UK Secretary of State for Education

'The Macat analyses provide immediate access to the critical conversation surrounding the books that have shaped their respective discipline, which will make them an invaluable resource to all of those, students and teachers, working in the field.'

Professor William Tronzo, University of California at San Diego

WAYS IN TO THE TEXT

KEY POINTS

- David Hume (1711–76) was a Scottish philosopher.

- Published in 1748, Hume's *An Enquiry Concerning Human Understanding* is an account of the origins of our beliefs about the world.

- It is one of the greatest works of the British empiricist* tradition in philosophy.

Who was David Hume?

David Hume was born in the Scottish city of Edinburgh in 1711 to an aristocratic, if not very wealthy, family. A scholarly young man, Hume entered the University of Edinburgh at the age of 12. He left without a degree, however, and could not get a position at a university in later years—partly because of his religious views. Hume did not accept Christianity. Indeed, he arguably did not believe in God at all, and as the Church of Scotland* controlled Scottish universities, someone with his religious views would not have been seen as a model employee.

He became a diplomat and a writer instead. Soon, many saw him as a leading figure in the Scottish Enlightenment,* a period during which science and literature flourished in Scotland. Hume knew many leading intellectuals in Edinburgh, London and Paris, and spent time in rural France working on his philosophical writings. His first published work, *A Treatise of Human Nature,* in which he presented his theory of the human mind, appeared in 1738. Its sales were slow at first, so Hume wrote a shorter, more popular introduction to his ideas—*An Enquiry Concerning Human Understanding.* In 1754 he gained fame as the author of the hugely popular *History of England.*

In his later years, Hume wrote a book arguing against belief in God. It was published as *Dialogues Concerning Natural Religion* after his death in Edinburgh in 1776; the book's subject was considered so highly controversial that Hume chose to publish it posthumously.

Although many think Hume was the greatest philosopher ever to write in English, he was best known during his lifetime as a historian. He was the last great figure in the philosophical movement called British empiricism, which emphasized the importance of experience in human thought and knowledge.

What Does *An Enquiry Concerning Human Understanding* Say?

Through his philosophy, Hume attempted to understand something that science had not yet explained: the workings of the human mind. While contemporary science had made great progress in understanding the world, the mind still remained largely unexplored. Hume set out to change that, using scientific principles to explore the ways we think about the act of thinking.

In Hume's view, many of our beliefs about the world stem neither from experience nor reason but from the way our minds work. In short, we have the beliefs we do because of human nature.

Hume begins his argument with an empiricist principle that everything in the mind is either an impression* or an idea.* By "impression" he means, roughly, a sense experience. An "idea" is a copy of an impression. Suppose, for example, that you see a red apple. In seeing the apple you gain an impression of it. But when you call it to mind, even just a moment later, what you remember is an idea copied from the impression.

Hume points out that we make sense of our experience by believing that one thing causes another. But our belief in this idea of what is called "causation" does not itself derive from any experience; according to Hume, it comes from certain habits of mind. We are in the habit of expecting the future to be like the past, for example. But this habit is not justified by experience; we create it because it is our human nature to do so.

This lead Hume to the issue of skepticism,* the school of philosophy that believes true knowledge is impossible. If our beliefs about the world do not come from experience, Hume argues, then why would we have those beliefs? Can we know anything about the world? According to Hume, philosophical reasoning suggests we cannot. However, people need to form beliefs about the world in order to live their lives. Belief in causation—one thing causing another—is too central to human nature to be undermined by a philosophical argument.

Hume was influenced by previous philosophers, especially the British empiricist John Locke.* Locke believed that sense experiences—thoughts, perceptions or emotions—produce ideas, and we hold those ideas in the mind. We cannot know a color, for example, unless we have seen it. In Locke's view, we can understand everything in the mind, including beliefs, by asking what experiences caused them.

Later philosophers like Immanuel Kant* saw Hume as pushing empiricism to its logical conclusion: if empiricism is a valid method of understanding things, if every idea must be tested and verified scientifically, then we cannot have any genuine knowledge of the world. These philosophers saw Hume as unintentionally demonstrating that empiricism cannot be valid because its logical conclusion is skepticism, and skepticism is absurd because there are things one can know with certainty. I know my name, for example, and that London is the capital of Britain. In the mid-twentieth century, the philosopher Bertrand Russell* noted that Hume's philosophical reasoning leads to "a dead end; in his direction, it is impossible to go further."

More recent students of Hume have interpreted him differently, and understand him as not showing that knowledge is either possible or impossible at all. According to them, Hume is, in fact, practicing psychology, showing how the mind works. Hume does not ask whether our beliefs are true or false. He asks, rather, why we have them and where they come from. [1]

Why Does *An Enquiry Concerning Human Understanding* Matter?

Hume's arguments resonate throughout subsequent thinking in philosophy, psychology and science. Their historical importance cannot be denied.

The history of psychology sees Hume's arguments as pioneering attempts to understand the human mind by using scientific methods. Although later psychologists adopted more complex models of the mind, Hume's theory of the mind was an influential early attempt.

In the discipline of philosophy, Hume contributed to epistemology,* or the study of knowledge. He asked how it was possible for human beings to gain knowledge and showed that our beliefs about the world are less secure than we would like to think— experience alone cannot account for them.

Hume also challenged belief in the existence of God, arguing that we have no good reason to believe that God exists or that miracles* occur. These are fundamental issues, still being debated.

Today, we often see science as the best way to understand the world and advance knowledge. Hume would agree—he was an early advocate of the scientific world view. But we think of science as based on evidence; Hume challenges that assumption. For him, evidence alone cannot account for scientific beliefs—there is always a gap between the evidence and scientific claims. Philosophers and scientists who want to understand science itself must confront Hume's arguments.

More generally, Hume's approach offers a good way to challenge our own beliefs about the world. Hume always asks where our beliefs come from and why we hold them. He looks for the roots of our beliefs in our experience of the world. He teaches us a critical method that can be applied to every belief. Even if we disagree with Hume's conclusions, we can use his methods to test our beliefs.

Hume's *Enquiry* is also a beautifully written book, well worth reading just for his prose style. It is clear evidence of the reason many regard Hume as one of the greatest philosophical writers.

NOTES

1   Bertrand Russell, *History of Western Philosophy* (London: Routledge, 2004), 600.

SECTION 1
INFLUENCES

MODULE 1
THE AUTHOR AND THE
HISTORICAL CONTEXT

KEY POINTS

- *An Enquiry Concerning Human Understanding* is one of the most influential books ever written on the workings of the human mind.

- Hume came from a devout Christian background, but turned his back on religion when he was a young man to study philosophy, especially as it relates to the mind.

- He wrote during a period of great intellectual development known as the Scottish Enlightenment.*

Why Read this Text?

Many people regard David Hume's *An Enquiry Concerning Human Understanding*, published in 1748, as the best example of the British empiricist* tradition in philosophy. Empiricism is the view that all human knowledge comes from experience. Empiricists believed everything that exists in the mind comes from our senses; Hume traces the contents of the mind, and especially a person's beliefs, back to their roots in the experience of the senses.

Hume's conclusion aligns with skeptical* philosophy: the view that genuine knowledge of the world is impossible to attain. In Hume's opinion, experience cannot be the reason behind our beliefs about the world. Rather, the experiences we have result to a large degree from certain habits of mind. These habits may explain our beliefs, but do not provide a rational reason for them. Hume thinks we cannot help but have these beliefs because practical life would be impossible without them.

> ❝ I found a certain boldness of temper growing in me, which was not inclined to submit to any authority in these subjects, but led me to seek out some new medium, by which truth might be established. After much study and reflection on this, at last, when I was about 18 years of age, there seemed to be opened up to me a new scene of thought, which transported me beyond measure, and made me, with an ardor natural to young men, throw up every other pleasure or business to apply entirely to it. ❞
>
> David Hume, *A Kind of History of My Life*

This argument is important both to the philosophy of the mind and to the field of psychology. Hume offered a naturalistic* account of the mind. In philosophy, naturalism is the view that philosophy and science are both trying to understand life as it really is. When Hume was writing in the middle of the eighteenth century, scientists like Isaac Newton* had already made great progress in understanding the physical world. Hume hoped to extend this progress to the mind by applying scientific methods to its study.

Second, Hume's skeptical conclusions are important in epistemology,* the philosophical study of knowledge. Some commentators say that Hume's work shows that empiricism leads to absurd conclusions (specifically, the conclusion that we have no knowledge of causal relations—that is, the fact that one thing causes another). By arguing that all knowledge depends on sense experience, Hume unintentionally (these commentators believed) showed that empiricism must be false. The most important thinker to hold this view was the German philosopher Immanuel Kant,* whose work attempted to explain the relationship between the way people reason and the things they experience. Other people believe that Hume's skepticism reveals a fundamental problem facing human knowledge: that genuine knowledge of the world is impossible. The Austrian philosopher Karl Popper* was an important supporter of this view in the twentieth century.[1]

Author's Life

Hume was born into the minor Scottish gentry in Edinburgh in 1711. His parents, though comfortably off, were not particularly rich, so Hume was never able to live off the family estate; he had to work for a living. Educated at home by tutors, Hume became a voracious reader at a very young age. He went to the University of Edinburgh at just 12 years of age (most people started at 14) and studied there for four years, though he did not receive a degree.[2]

Hume decided to make his way in the world as an independent scholar. In later life he applied for academic positions at the University of Edinburgh and the University of Glasgow, but was turned down for both. This could be because his views about religion, mainly his doubts as to the existence of God, were regarded as unorthodox and dangerous.

Hume's first major work, *A Treatise of Human Nature,*[3] was published in three volumes in 1739 and 1740. A long book that failed to find many readers at first or make much of an impression on scholars, Hume famously said the *Treatise* "fell dead-born from the press."[4]

In an effort to attract a wider audience for his ideas, Hume published the shorter and more accessible *An Enquiry into Human Understanding* in 1748. By this time he was working as secretary to the Scottish soldier and politician Lieutenant-General James St Clair.* Hume became involved in politics and diplomacy himself, work that took him to great European cities like Vienna and Turin. He had many friends in intellectual circles in Edinburgh, in London and in France, where he lived for a time.[5]

Hume's six-volume *History of England* was published between

1754 and 1762 and became a bestseller, bringing him wealth and fame as a historian rather than as a philosopher. He died of a form of abdominal cancer in the city of his birth, Edinburgh, at the age of 65 in 1776.

Author's Background

The mid-eighteenth century in Hume's native Scotland was a time of great intellectual progress in science, philosophy and literature—so much so that the period has become known as the Scottish Enlightenment. Important figures of the time included the economist Adam Smith* (a personal friend of Hume's), the scientist James Hutton,* and James Watt,* who invented the modern steam engine. Moving in these circles, Hume lived and wrote in a cultured and open intellectual environment independent of the universities and religious authorities.

Like most Scots of the time, Hume's family practiced a strict and rigid form of Christianity. Hume himself said he was a religious child who took the teachings of Christianity very seriously. But while at university he read many philosophical and scientific works and seems to have abandoned religion. At the end of his life, Hume said that he had never truly believed in religion after reading the English philosophers John Locke* and Samuel Clarke.*[6] In his philosophical writings, Hume seems suspicious of religion in general and of Christianity in particular.

Because of his beliefs, some members of the clergy saw Hume as a radical. In this they were not wrong. Knowing that his views would displease some authorities and unwilling to risk having his entire body of work censored, Hume insisted that his last important philosophical writings, a discussion about religion and the existence of God, should not be published in his lifetime. *Dialogues Concerning Natural Religion*[7] appeared in 1779, three years after he died.

NOTES

1   Karl Popper, Conjectures and Refutations (London: Routledge, 2002), 55–61.

2   David Hume, "My Own Life," in The Cambridge Companion to Hume, ed. David Fate Norton (Cambridge: Cambridge University Press, 1993), 351.

3   Hume, A Treatise of Human Nature (Oxford: Oxford University Press, 1978).

4   Hume, "My Own Life," 352.

5   Hume, "My Own Life," 352–3.

6   James Boswell, "An account of my last interview with David Hume, Esq," in Boswell in Extremes 1776–1778, ed. Charles Weis and Frederick Pottle (New York: McGraw-Hill, 1970), 11.

7   Hume, Dialogues Concerning Natural Religion (Cambridge: Cambridge University Press, 2007).

MODULE 2
ACADEMIC CONTEXT

KEY POINTS

- Sir Isaac Newton* and other scientists transformed our understanding of the natural world in the seventeenth century.
- Philosophers and scientists aimed to use the methods of the new science to understand the human mind.
- Hume was influenced both by these efforts and by the ancient skeptical* tradition that had been revived by Pierre Bayle.*

The Work In Its Context

David Hume's *An Enquiry Concerning Human Understanding* capitalized on advances in natural science made by his predecessors in the seventeenth and eighteenth centuries. Isaac Newton's* system of physics, first published in 1687, set out a new conception of the physical world, heavily mathematical but based on rigorous empirical* (that is, evidence-based) testing. The new science launched a revolution in both methods and theories, using experiment and observation to test its results. It also described the world using very general principles, which it used to explain phenomena that had previously seemed very varied. Newton's law of universal gravitation, for example, explained both the motion of objects on the surface of the earth and the movements of the planets.

Thinkers of this era drew no clear distinctions between philosophy and science. The two were considered as a single discipline, divided into "natural philosophy"—the study of the natural world, including physics, astronomy, chemistry and biology—and "moral philosophy,"

> **❝** [Hume's work] aimed at no less than the destruction of the doctrine of the image of God, and substituted for it an anthropology which looked not to the divine but to the natural world for its comparisons, and to the sciences for its methods. Man was a natural object; not, as for Leibniz, a little god beside the great God, but a great animal among the lesser animals. **❞**
>
> Edward Craig, *The Mind of God and the Works of Man*

which concerned itself more specifically with human beings.

In the hands of scientists like Newton and Robert Boyle,* who is today generally recognized as one of the first practitioners of modern chemistry, the new scientific method had achieved great results in natural philosophy. It had not yet been applied in a sustained way to moral philosophy. Scholars began to dream of extending the new methods into the domain of human society and economics, and of human psychology.

Overview of the Field

The desire to study thought has a long history—perhaps as long as the history of thoughts themselves. In the seventeenth century, the French philosopher René Descartes* theorized about "the way of ideas." According to Descartes and his followers, "ideas" occur in our minds when we think, feel or perceive something. Introspection—the examination of our own mental processes—gives us direct access to those ideas. When I see a green patch of grass for example, or merely imagine or think of a green patch, I get an idea of greenness.

A century later, British empiricism* added to the mix the notion of applying newly expressed scientific principles to the study of the human mind. The empiricists believed that the contents of the mind come from sense experience; to them, ideas were mental representations of the outside world that arrive in the mind through the sense organs. Hume's most important influences in this tradition were the English philosopher John Locke* and the Irish philosopher George Berkeley.*

In tracing ideas back to sense experiences, Locke argued that the world is very different from our common-sense conception of it and that we can only discover the true nature of the world through natural science. Berkeley came to an even more radical conclusion, arguing that there is no material world at all: nothing exists except ideas and the minds in which ideas occur, including the mind of God.

Academic Influences

Hume was a keen reader of Descartes, Locke, Berkeley and the other philosophers who had contributed to the growing debate about the mind. But he was also influenced by other intellectual trends in his time, like the revival of interest in an ancient Greek school of thought called Pyrrhonian skepticism.* This tradition was repopularized by the French philosopher Pierre Bayle,* who gained fame with a book of essays called the *Historical and Critical Dictionary* (1697), a work Hume often mentioned.

Pyrrhonian skeptics thought that truth was not accessible to human beings: Since we are always liable to error, we should suspend judgment. Instead of trying to find out about the world, skeptics believed that we should just live according to our natural instincts.

Bayle popularized skepticism, but not by putting forward a general principle that knowledge is impossible. Instead, he examined many different systems of belief, including religious beliefs—finding each uncertain and open to doubt. In this way Bayle emphasized the limitations of human reason. Bayle concluded, among other things, that since the human mind is always liable to make mistakes, we should tolerate different opinions. In particular, he argued, we should not persecute other people's religions.

MODULE 3
THE PROBLEM

KEY POINTS

- Philosophers and scientists asked how the mind worked; in particular, where our ideas come from and why we have them.

- The seventeenth-century philosopher John Locke argued that ideas are caused by external objects; the Irish philosopher George Berkeley rejected this view and claimed that there are no external objects.

- Hume attempted to offer general principles that explain why some ideas give rise to others.

Core Question

Eighteenth-century philosophers explored the question of how the mind works. David Hume's *An Enquiry Concerning Human Understanding* fits squarely into this tradition.

Hume's contemporaries believed that the contents of the mind are made up of ideas—the mental "objects" that come into being when we have a thought. A principal question they asked was how and why ideas give rise to other ideas. If we understood that, they thought, we would understand the principles that govern the operations of the mind.

Philosophers of this period understood all mental states and operations in terms of ideas. Centrally, this includes sense perceptions and beliefs. But it also includes memories, emotions, pleasure and pain, and all other aspects of our mental lives. In each case, philosophers asked where these ideas came from, and how one idea may cause another to occur.

They also asked a related question: Do our ideas represent the world accurately? In sense experience, for example, do we see the

> **❝** The understanding, like the eye, while it makes us see, and perceive all other things, takes no notice of itself. And it requires art and pains to set it at a distance, and make it its own object. **❞**
>
> Thomas Paine, *Common Sense* John Locke, *An Essay Concerning Human Understanding*

world as it really is? Are our beliefs about the world true?

So the issue was in part a psychological one about how the mind works and in part an epistemological* one, about whether and how we can gain genuine knowledge of the world.

The Participants

Hume's most important predecessors in the tradition of British empiricism* were John Locke and George Berkeley. Both of these thinkers adopted the view that all our ideas originate in sense experience. Just as one could not think of a color—or imagine it, or remember it—without having first seen the color, they thought the same was true of all our ideas.

Both thinkers went on to ask if our ideas indeed resemble the external world at all. When I see a green patch, for example, does my idea of green correspond to a green patch that really exists in the world? Here, Locke and Berkeley differ.

Locke believed that ideas are caused by an external objects. If you look at a green cup, for example, then the cup is the cause of your idea of green.

Nevertheless, Locke thought, that idea is not *exactly like* the object. For example, the color green you see does not actually exist in the physical world. Your idea of the color depends on different textures in the outside world that reflect light of different wavelengths. So, although the ideas we hold are caused by the external world, they do not always resemble it.

The view that there is an external world for ideas to correspond to is known as "realism."* Berkeley went against realism, instead putting forward an alternative view, often called "idealism."* According to Berkeley, we have no reason to suppose there is any external world corresponding to our ideas. After all, we cannot see such a world directly. When we try to compare our ideas with the world, we can only do so using sense experience, in the process creating further ideas.

The Contemporary Debate

Hume was influenced by both Locke and Berkeley (Locke, to whom he often refers by name, especially). He was not, however, satisfied with Locke's practice of referring to all the objects of thought and perception as "ideas." He thought that doing so overlooked important distinctions.

In particular, Hume distinguished between the objects of sense experience and the objects of thought (including the objects of imagination and memory, and so on). He called the objects of sense experience "impressions," and the others "ideas." Hume expressed the empiricist principle that everything in the mind comes from the senses in this way: all ideas are copies of impressions.[1]

Hume also wanted to explain why certain ideas occur in the mind. Suppose that, whenever I smell coffee, I think of the taste of coffee. One idea (the smell of coffee) has given rise to another (the taste of coffee). Hume wanted to formulate a few general principles that would show why one idea often follows another.

Hume is sometimes thought of as an idealist, like Berkeley. But when it comes to the question of whether our ideas correspond to external objects, Hume is neither an idealist nor a realist: He is simply not interested. Instead, he is interested in the ideas themselves, and in particular in why one idea causes another to occur.

NOTES

1   David Hume, *An Enquiry Concerning Human Understanding* (Cambridge: Cambridge University Press, 2007), 14–15.

MODULE 4
THE AUTHOR'S CONTRIBUTION

KEY POINTS

- Hume argued that many of our beliefs about the world are not based on reason.

- He both explained the workings of human reason and showed its limitations.

- Other philosophers of the time explained the origins of our beliefs—for example, our moral beliefs—by reference to emotion rather than to reason.

Author's Aims

David Hume describes his *An Enquiry Concerning Human Understanding* as dealing with "the science of human nature,"[1] an attempt to explain facts about the human mind. Since he considers human beings as reasoning and believing, he wishes to explain why we think about the world as we do. This project has both positive and negative aspects. On one hand, it involves achieving a new scientific understanding of the mind. But on the other hand the project casts doubt on much of what human beings believe, since it argues that many of our beliefs—such as religious or philosophical beliefs—have no basis in reason. Thus the project encourages a sort of skepticism,* the view that genuine knowledge of the world is impossible.

Enquiry has struck many, from Immanuel Kant* onwards, as an extremely consistent application of empiricist* principles to the study of the mind. Hume follows his argument to its conclusions, even if those conclusions (like that of skepticism) can seem strange and disturbing. Skepticism suggests that our ordinary, everyday beliefs have no grounding in reality, so that a true understanding of the world will forever be beyond our grasp. Some have even taken Hume to have

> **❝** Reason is and ought only to be the slave of the passions, and can never pretend to any other office than to serve and obey them. **❞**
>
> David Hume, *A Treatise of Human Nature*

unintentionally undermined empiricism by pushing it to its logical conclusion, showing that if empiricism is true, then skepticism must also be true.

The issue of skepticism can, however, become a barrier to understanding Hume's project. Hume's main aim is not to *change* our beliefs about the world, but rather to *understand* them. His primary interest is psychology—the study of mental processes—not epistemology, the study of knowledge itself. To present Hume primarily as a destructive philosopher who wishes to undermine beliefs that he argues are not grounded in reason distorts his intentions. Indeed, at the end of *Enquiry* Hume suggests that, for the purposes of ordinary life, one can accept his argument without destroying one's world view. Hume accepts that it is natural for human beings to form beliefs that cannot be rationally justified. For example, when I hear birdsong I almost automatically form the belief that there are birds nearby, and no philosophical argument can stop me from forming that belief. That's just part of human nature. Hume does not argue that there is anything wrong with forming beliefs that go beyond the evidence, or that we should cease to do so.

Approach

David Hume undertook a scientific investigation of human nature, and in particular of the human mind. He wanted to understand how the mind works, and why human beings think as we do. In particular, he aimed to identify the basic principles that govern the operations of the mind. Not content with observing and recording various mental phenomena, he sought to identify the mind's most general features.

In the opening chapter of his *Enquiry*, Hume defended his project, noting that the question is not just interesting, but is *essential* to answer.[2] People need an accurate and well-grounded picture of human nature to achieve their aims and cultivate a good life.

Hume also puts forward a different justification for his interest. It is part of human nature that people will always attempt to understand the world, even if it means asking perplexing and difficult theoretical questions that may well be beyond the capacity of the human mind to answer. Understanding the limits of the human mind would help us to work out which questions our mental abilities are capable of answering, and those that are not. In this way, the success of Hume's project would mean defining the boundaries of the human intellect.

Contribution In Context

Hume regarded his theory of the mind as his life's work. He first proposed this theory in his three-volume work *A Treatise of Human Nature*, but its reception disappointed him. He intended the *Enquiry* to be a shorter, more accessible introduction to some of his principal ideas.

Hume's approach to psychology had a predecessor in the work of Francis Hutcheson,* a Scottish philosopher who was something of a mentor to Hume. Hutcheson's interests lay particularly in the fields of morality (the principles behind right and wrong) and aesthetics (the principles concerned with nature and beauty). He explained that our judgments about morality and about beauty did not stem from reasoning but from what he called the "sentiments"—what we would call today "emotions." On this point, Hume agreed with Hutcheson. But Hume went further. He argued that reason was less important than was often thought, not only in morals and aesthetics but also in our other beliefs about the world, including those about nature.

Hutcheson exchanged letters with Hume on philosophical matters, and Hume admired him enormously, but the friendship soured when

Hutcheson opposed Hume's application for a post at the University of Edinburgh because of Hume's views on religion, an action he found hugely disappointing.[3]

NOTES

1   David Hume, *An Enquiry Concerning Human Understanding* (Cambridge: Cambridge University Press, 2007), 3.

2   Hume, *Enquiry*, 3–13.

3   James Moore, "Hutcheson and Hume," in *Hume and Hume's Connexions*, ed. M. A. Stewart and John P. Wright (Edinburgh: Edinburgh University Press, 1990), 23–57.

SECTION 2
IDEAS

MODULE 5
MAIN IDEAS

KEY POINTS

- Hume makes a distinction between two sorts of questioning: Relations of ideas and matters of fact. Relations of ideas have to do mostly with mathematics; matters of fact concern the external world and our knowledge of them requires observation and experiment.

- Hume argues that our beliefs about causal relations—the idea that one thing leads to another—rest on mental habits rather than on observation.

- The *Enquiry* is a briefer and more accessible introduction to ideas explained in his earlier three-volume *Treatise of Human Nature*.

Key Themes

David Hume, in his *An Enquiry Concerning Human Understanding*, argues that human beings engage in two sorts of inquiry, or questioning: "matters of fact"* and "relations of ideas."*[1]

The second kind of inquiry, about how ideas relate to each other, can only be accomplished by using reason. And Hume believes its only valid use lies in one discipline: mathematics. In his view, everything outside of mathematics must rely on facts gained by conducting research and experiments. Books of metaphysics or theology that do not draw on experimental results can only contain "sophistry* and illusion"—false arguments and imagined truths. He urges us to "commit [such works], then, to the flames."[2]

The first sort of inquiry he defines—for "matters of fact" about anything in the natural world—requires empirical research and experiments. Unfortunately, Hume notes, humans have a habit of abandoning empirical knowledge and instead basing reasoning about

> **❝** Custom, then, is the great guide of human life. It
> is that principle alone which renders our experience
> useful to us, and makes us expect, for the future, a
> similar train of events with those that have appeared in
> the past. **❞**
>
> David Hume, *An Enquiry Concerning Human Understanding*

matters of fact on observation. But observation by itself cannot explain
why we hold the beliefs we do. We often believe things that mere
observation cannot justify, particularly in regard to the external world.
Hume traces this to our beliefs about causation.

Exploring The Ideas

When Hume writes that "All reasonings concerning matters of fact
seem to be founded on the relation of *Cause and Effect*,"[3] he is arguing
that our knowledge of the external world depends on our beliefs
about causal relations—how one event will cause another event to
occur. When I hear the sound of raindrops on the window and
conclude that it is raining, for instance, I am using my knowledge of
the fact that rain causes that sound.

However, Hume argues that experience is never enough to justify
the belief that one event *has* caused another. All we can actually
understand is that events succeed each other with a certain regularity
and predictability. On the basis of experience alone, we can never
reach the conclusion that one event happened *because of* another.
Suppose that, watching a game of pool, I see one ball hitting another,
causing it to move. Hume thinks that, strictly speaking, all I see when
this occurs is that both balls move, not that the first ball caused the
movement of the second. In the terms of Hume's empiricism,* we do
not have any understanding of causal relations between the two pool
balls.

Why then do we hold beliefs about causation? We do so because our minds are governed by what he calls "custom and habit": custom, Hume says, is "the great guide of human life."[4] When we notice a "constant conjunction" between two different events—for example, the first pool ball hitting the second, and the second beginning to move—we automatically expect that the next time we observe pool balls the same thing will occur. Anyone who has tried to learn the game can confirm that this is not always the case.

Having noticed certain patterns (that fire is hot, say, or that snow is cold), we are naturally inclined to expect those patterns to continue to be the same in the future, even though we can never *show* that they will. We expect regularity, not because we have empirical evidence of such regularity, but rather because it is in our nature to expect patterns to repeat. One conclusion Hume draws is that we have no good reason to expect the future to be like the past. Just because we have always found snow to be cold, it does not follow that we will continue to find it cold in the future.

Language And Expression

Although Hume had expressed his main argument in an earlier work, he later wrote of it that he "had always entertained a notion, that my want of success in publishing the *Treatise of Human Nature*, had proceeded more from the manner than the matter."[5] If he had written the *Treatise* in too obscure a voice, Hume thought that a shorter, easier-to-read version would attract a greater audience. And although he was right, the work did not gain a wide readership until after his death.

A beautifully written book, *Enquiry* has helped win Hume a reputation as one of the best writers of philosophical prose in the English language, if not *the* best. Although its language is by now old-fashioned, it still remains accessible to modern readers, attractively written in relatively simple English.

Enquiry's success may have influenced the way Hume has been interpreted. Readers sometimes think of Hume as mostly interested in epistemological* questions (that is, investigating the origin, nature and limits of human knowledge) and particularly questions about skepticism.* The three-volume *Treatise* makes it clear that this is only part of Hume's concerns. His aim—to formulate a theory of the human mind—is much broader, and skepticism is only one of the issues that arises from that project. In general, Hume's interests are more psychological, as his readers would see if they tackled the more comprehensive *Treatise*.

NOTES

1 David Hume, *An Enquiry Concerning Human Understanding* (Cambridge: Cambridge University Press, 2007), 28.

2 Hume, *Enquiry*, 144.

3 Hume, *Enquiry*, 29.

4 Hume, *Enquiry*, 45.

5 David Hume, "My Own Life," in *The Cambridge Companion to Hume*, ed. David Fate Norton (Cambridge: Cambridge University Press, 1993), 352.

MODULE 6
SECONDARY IDEAS

KEY POINTS

- Hume argued against believing accounts of miracles, and against the view that, since God is good, there is an afterlife that compensates for the evils of this life.

- Hume's arguments concerning religion were very controversial.

- The argument against belief in miracles has been influential both in philosophy of religion and in epistemology.*

Other Ideas

In the later chapters of *An Enquiry Concerning Human Understanding*, David Hume makes skeptical* arguments about religion in general, and in particular about the Christian religion, which was dominant in Europe when the book was published in 1748. While perhaps not the principal point of the book, these arguments have nevertheless proven very influential.

First, Hume tackles the issue of miracles.[1] Christians argued that many miracles had occurred in the early history of the Church, as recorded in lives of the saints and other contemporary sources. The question arises of whether such sources are trustworthy. If they are to be believed, they seem to offer good reason to accept Christianity.

Hume argues, however, that the reports are not trustworthy because they cannot be scientifically verified. As a good empiricist, Hume argues that testimony,* even that of a saint, should be accepted only when it is the same as our own first-hand experience of the world. Further, Hume says, given that Christianity "cannot be believed

> 66 We may conclude, that the Christian religion not only was at first attended with miracles, but even at this day cannot be believed by any reasonable person without one. Mere reason is insufficient to convince us of its veracity; and whoever is moved by faith to assent to it, is conscious of a continued miracle in his own person, which subverts all the principles of his understanding, and gives him a determination to believe what is most contrary to custom and experience. 99
>
> David Hume, *Natural History of Religion*

by any reasonable person"[2] without a miracle, one must doubt the truth of Christianity itself.

Second, Hume addresses the Christian notion of the perfect power and goodness of God.[3] He does not make this argument in his own voice, but, rather, uses the literary device of reporting a conversation he supposedly had with a friend. It may be that Hume was wary of identifying himself with the conclusion of the argument, given its radical and anti-establishment implications. Christians believed that, since God is infinitely good and powerful, we have reason to believe that the imperfections and evils of this world will be compensated for in the afterlife. Hume argues against this idea.

Exploring The Ideas

In Hume's definition, a miracle is not merely an unusual or surprising event. It is a suspension of the laws of nature, during which regularities in nature that have otherwise always been observed to be true seem to break down. So a miracle, by definition, is an event of a sort that has always been observed not to occur. In this circumstance, Hume argues, it is more reasonable to suppose that testimony of miracles is false (whether because the reporters were innocently mistaken, or distorted the feat through misinterpretation, or purposefully intended to deceive) than to believe that miracles have actually occurred.

"No testimony is sufficient to establish a miracle," Hume writes, "unless the testimony be of such a kind that its falsehood would be more miraculous than the fact which it endeavors to establish."[4]

Following Hume's view that all beliefs should be based on empirical* evidence, we can only believe that God is powerful and good to the extent that the evidence suggests that is true. Christians make a mistake when they suppose that, for example, there must be some reason for evils in the world, whether or not we can discover the reason. Similarly, they are mistaken when they argue that given the imperfect nature of the world, there must be a better afterlife. In holding these beliefs, Hume argues, they assume that God is more perfect than the evidence warrants.

These arguments, highly radical and original in Hume's time, had enormous influence in subsequent efforts to arrive at a rational and evidence-based appraisal of religious belief. In the case of the argument concerning miracles, Hume has been influential in another way, especially in recent times. The argument has become a classic text in debates about the epistemology* of testimony: that is, the use of the word of others, whether spoken or written, as a source of knowledge.[5]

Overlooked

An Enquiry Concerning Human Understanding is a short work that has been intensively studied for over two centuries. Every section of the book has received a great deal of attention. Nevertheless, especially until recently, certain aspects of it have been relatively overlooked. One of these is the depth of Hume's engagement with the ancient Greek tradition of skepticism.* Skepticism had often featured in philosophy as a challenge, with philosophers seeking to refute the skeptic by proving that knowledge is possible. But Hume found another attitude in the Greek tradition: skepticism as a positive vision of how to live.

Hume showed that while many of our beliefs are not based entirely on reason, they are the products of non-rational aspects of human nature: the emotions, for example, and our animal instincts and expectations. He did not see this as a problem to be put right. He recognized that reason alone can never be enough to ground a world view—we could never rebuild our belief system based solely on reason. Instead, Hume felt that we should simply accept the fundamentally non-rational basis of many of our beliefs. This parallels the thinking of the Pyrrhonian* skeptics, followers of the ancient Greek philosopher Pyrrho of Elis. Pyrrhonian skeptics believed that since human beings were not capable of acquiring knowledge, we should suspend judgment about the ways the world is and act according to our natural instincts rather than our beliefs.

Hume differs from the ancient skeptics, however. At the end of *Enquiry* he writes: "The great subverter of Pyrrhonism or the excessive principles of scepticism is action, and employment, and the occupations of common life."[6] He thought that it is part of human nature to believe, and one cannot live life without forming beliefs. Hume recommends leaving skeptical concerns behind in everyday life: not because they have been disproved, but because we must ignore them for practical purposes.

NOTES

1   David Hume, *An Enquiry Concerning Human Understanding* (Cambridge: Cambridge University Press, 2007), 96–116.

2   Hume, *Enquiry*, 116.

3   Hume, *Enquiry*, 117–130.

4   Hume, *Enquiry*, 101.

5   See the essays in *The Epistemology of Testimony*, ed. Jennifer Lackey and Ernest Sosa (Oxford: Oxford University Press, 2006).

6   Hume, *Enquiry*, 139–140.

MODULE 7
ACHIEVEMENT

KEY POINTS

- Hume's skeptical* arguments, especially those about causation and belief in miracles, have been widely studied and accepted.

- Later philosophers often found inspiration for their own projects in Hume's writings.

- Especially since the work of German philosopher Immanuel Kant* in the late eighteenth century, Hume has been read as making a skeptical challenge to knowledge. His larger project, of formulating a theory of the human mind, has sometimes been ignored.

Assessing The Argument

David Hume pursues both philosophy and psychology in *An Enquiry Concerning Human Understanding*. On the one hand, the project is epistemological.* Hume the philosopher assesses certain claims we make about our knowledge (those about causes and effects, or about miracles, for example). He is broadly skeptical of these claims, showing how weak our reasons for making them are.

On the other hand, Hume the scientist puts forward a psychological theory about of the workings of the mind. He is interested in explaining why our minds work as they do, and why we believe what we believe. He is not interested in assessing our beliefs; he wants to explain them.

There is reason to think that formulating a theory of the mind is in fact Hume's main purpose in writing the *Enquiry*. He wrote the book as a brief introduction to the ideas articulated in his *Treatise of Human*

> ❝David Hume is one of the most important among philosophers, because he developed to its logical conclusion the empirical philosophy of Locke and Berkeley, and by making it self-consistent made it incredible. He represents, in a certain sense, a dead end: in his direction, it is impossible to go further. ❞
> Bertrand Russell,* *History of Western Philosophy*

Nature, describing it as "an attempt to introduce the experimental method of reasoning into moral subjects." In short, the *Treatise* was an attempt to apply scientific reasoning to the study of human beings.

Hume's arguments about causal belief and belief in miracles have been very influential. Everyone who writes about these topics today must confront his position. Indeed, many have thought that Hume is clearly correct in his arguments on these topics. The twentieth century Australian philosopher J. L. Mackie,* for example, argued this point in his well-known book *The Miracle of Theism*.[1] Paradoxically, the very success and prominence of Hume's arguments has often caused people to lose sight of his overall psychological project. His arguments in psychology may have been more important to him than his arguments in epistemology* (that is, his theory of knowledge). But it is the latter which have had the most lasting influence.

Achievement In Context

In the nineteenth and early twentieth centuries, many commentators, influenced by the German philosopher Immanuel Kant,* took Hume to be primarily a skeptic who provided a challenge to our established beliefs about the world. The role of the post-Humean philosopher was to find out whether these beliefs could be defended against the criticisms leveled at Hume.

But from the mid-twentieth century on, it became more common to see Hume primarily as a naturalist* philosopher (a philosopher who believes that only natural laws affect the behavior of the universe). The most influential early champion of this view was probably Hume's fellow Scotsman Norman Kemp Smith,* the author of *The Philosophy of David Hume.*[2] In it, Kemp Smith argued that Hume intended to investigate the human mind according to the principles of natural science, and so understood human beings as part of the natural world.

If scholars have found it difficult to interpret some of Hume's ideas, a good example might be his ideas about causation. Hume argues that we tend to see events as causing each other because of the structure of our minds, rather than any observable evidence. But this leads us to a contentious question: Is Hume simply describing the processes by which humans form beliefs? Or is he expressing skepticism* about whether causal processes exist at all?

For many years, Hume was seen as challenging philosophers to provide a rational justification for our ordinary beliefs about causation. But more recently an alternative interpretation has become popular through books such as *The Secret Connexion* by the British analytic philosopher Galen Strawson.* According to this interpretation, Hume was not casting doubt on the existence of causation but was investigating a completely separate topic altogether, and his psychological explanations of how our beliefs arise work independently of whether those beliefs are true or false.

Limitations

The interpretation of *Enquiry* has shifted greatly over time and, in some ways, from place to place, too. But interest in the book has not waned; no matter where they live, readers across the centuries have found something in it. Readers often see Hume's work as reflecting their own interests and ideas. The early twentieth century, for example, saw the rise of logical empiricism, or logical positivism,* a movement that shared Hume's belief that the only valid facts were those that could be scientifically verified. For the logical positivists, Hume was a forerunner. Later, naturalist philosophers reinterpeted Hume as believing that philosophy and science are engaged in the same project and use essentially the same methods.*

Philosophers in continental Europe have often popularized views different from those of their counterparts in Britain and North America, so it's not surprising that they differ on their interpretation of Hume and his importance to the discipline. The German phenomenologist* Edmund Husserl,* in his book *The Crisis of European Sciences*,[3] interprets Hume as showing the "bankruptcy" of empiricist* philosophy by reducing it to absurdity. Hume's argument shows how empiricism leads to skepticism* and solipsism*—the belief that the only thing one can know for certain is oneself.* If experience is the sole source of knowledge, we cannot be sure that the external world or even other people exist. Husserl believed that Hume's work demonstrated the need for a new start in philosophy that would avoid these absurd results.

In his *Empiricism and Subjectivity*,[4] the French philosopher Gilles Deleuze* claims Hume as a predecessor by interpreting him as an anti-foundationalist* (that is, someone who believes that philosophy should not attempt to find anything more certain or basic than our immediate experience of ourselves and of the world). Deleuze admired Hume's denial of metaphysical foundations (what is there and what is it like?) for both the self and for knowledge.

NOTES

1 J. L. Mackie, *The Miracle of Theism: Arguments For and Against the Existence of God* (Oxford: Oxford University Press, 1982).

2 Norman Kemp Smith, *The Philosophy of David Hume* (London: Macmillan, 1941).

3 Edmund Husserl, *The Crisis of the European Sciences and Transcendental Phenomenology*, trans. David Carr (Evanston: Northwestern University Press, 1970).

4 Gilles Deleuze, *Empiricism and Subjectivity*, trans. Constantin V. Boundas (New York: Columbia University Press, 1991).

MODULE 8
PLACE IN THE AUTHOR'S WORK

KEY POINTS

- Hume aimed throughout his life to construct a science of human nature.

- *Enquiry* restates many of the views that Hume had published in his earlier, three-volume *Treatise of Human Nature.*

- Hume's reputation is now based largely on the *Enquiry* and volume one of the *Treatise.*

Positioning

When David Hume published *An Enquiry Concerning Human Understanding* he was 37 years old and had not yet gained any fame as an author. By his own account, his philosophy began to take shape when he was still a teenager, and, in fact, he had put forward many of *Enquiry's* arguments and theories a decade earlier in *A Treatise of Human Nature,* a work he began writing when he was only 23.

The *Treatise* is a long and difficult work that was not widely read when it was first published. Hume hoped that the shorter and more accessible *Enquiry* would win his ideas a wider audience, which it did—but not until after Hume's death. The only widespread fame Hume won during his lifetime came from his writings on history and his essays for popular audiences, not from his philosophical work.

Hume never changed his mind about the basic nature of his philosophical project, nor about his most important conclusions: Early and late, he wanted to construct a science of human nature as a systematic explanation of human beings as thinking, feeling and acting creatures. The *Treatise* was an attempt to cover the whole of this vast

> **❝** Never literary attempt was more unfortunate than my *Treatise of Human Nature*. It fell dead-born from the press, without even reaching such distinction, as even to excite a murmur among the zealots. **❞**
>
> David Hume, "My Own Life"

field. In the shorter *Enquiry*, Hume focused his attention more narrowly on human understanding, and in particular on human beings as believing and knowing subjects. He asks why we believe what we believe.

Integration

The results Hume reaches in both the *Treatise* and *Enquiry* were important to all his philosophical writings. Reason played a limited role in his explanations of human nature. In Hume's view, much of what we do and think results from our nature, not just as reasoning beings, but as beings with emotions and instincts and expectations that have nothing to do with rationality.

This view leads to skepticism* about certain beliefs, especially those about religion: Hume doubts that we hold the religious beliefs we do because we are persuaded by arguments or evidence. In the absence of such evidence, Hume saw no reason to hold religious beliefs. But that was a very controversial argument in the eighteenth century—indeed, it will still raise hackles in some circles today. So Hume chose to omit many of his religious arguments from the *Treatise*. Later in his life he argued against a belief in God, especially in his last work, *Dialogues Concerning Natural Religion*, a book so controversial that he said it should not be published until after his death.

Another conclusion Hume reaches is the importance of the emotions—or, as Hume called them, the "sentiments"—in our mental lives. This led him to views about morality (the principles behind right and wrong) and aesthetics (the principles concerned with nature and beauty) that he expressed in other writings, including a very popular volume of *Essays*. In the important essay "Of the Standard of Taste," published in 1757, Hume argued that when we make judgments about beauty, we base them on sentiment rather than objective reality. So those judgments reflect nothing more than the nature of the human being who makes them.[1]

Significance

The *Enquiry* is one of Hume's most important and enduringly popular works. Along with Book One of the *Treatise*, with which it has a lot in common, it is the definitive statement of Hume's ideas about human understanding and knowledge. Hume's only comparably important philosophical works are Books Two and Three of the *Treatise*, in which he deals with the emotions and morality respectively.

In other words, Hume's reputation as one of the most important philosophers in the western tradition largely depends on two works: *Enquiry* and the *Treatise*.

Almost every section of *Enquiry* has given rise to philosophical debate. The sections on knowledge and skepticism are considered classics of epistemology.* The section on miracles has been important in the philosophy of religion, just as the discussion of free will has been important in metaphysics.* Perhaps most importantly of all, the section on our knowledge of causal relations has given rise to the problem of induction,* a central problem in the philosophy of science. Induction is the process of finding general principles on the basis of particular observations. It is usually regarded as a crucial element of scientific discovery.

There is also a lively debate on how to interpret Hume correctly. Despite the clarity of his writing style, there is considerable disagreement on the meaning and purpose of his overall project, with philosophers in each period seeming to find their own version of Hume.

NOTES

1   David Hume, *Essays Moral, Political, Literary* (Indianapolis: Liberty Classics, 1985).

SECTION 3
IMPACT

MODULE 9
THE FIRST RESPONSES

KEY POINTS

- Critics attacked Hume's theory of ideas and his account of causation.

- Hume countered that his critics believed in "innate ideas." This was tantamount to calling them old-fashioned thinkers.

- Kant and others felt that Hume's philosophy leads to skepticism,* and must be countered if skepticism is to be avoided.

Criticism

Few philosophers read and responded to David Hume's arguments in *An Enquiry Concerning Human Understanding* during his lifetime. The most important thinker to do so was another Scottish philosopher, Thomas Reid,* in his book *Inquiry into the Human Mind on the Principles of Common Sense,* first published in 1764.[1]

Reid argued against the basic assumption of Hume's philosophy (what Reid called "the way of ideas"). Other important thinkers of the period, John Locke* and George Berkeley* among them, also shared this assumption. According to Hume and others who supported the way of ideas, we never perceive and think of things in the external world directly; instead, we only form mental entities or ideas of them. For example: when I see an orange ball, my mind forms an idea of a circular orange object. What I see is this idea, not the physical ball. The mind does not touch external objects themselves.

Reid argued that this was a mistake. In his view the mind is not made up of *ideas* (that is, things we see, or think of) but of *activities*, the

> **❝** I freely admit the remembrance of David Hume was the very thing that many years ago first interrupted my dogmatic slumber and gave a completely different direction to my researches in the field of speculative philosophy. **❞**
>
> Immanuel Kant, *Prolegomena to Any Future Metaphysics*

acts of seeing and thinking. Typically, the objects of our seeing and thinking exist as physical objects outside the mind. So Reid would say that I directly perceive the orange ball; the ball does not reach my mind via an idea or any other intermediary.

Hume argued that human beings base our belief in causal relations merely on observations of regularity in nature; Reid replied that such observations cannot provide the basis of an adequate account of causation. We regularly observe that day follows night, but we do not believe that night causes the day. Further, sometimes we observe a singular example of causation. For instance, if I see a bird fly into and crack a window, I conclude that the bird caused the window to crack, even though I've never seen a bird crack a window before and perhaps never will again. In Reid's view causation cannot be understood in terms of regularly observed patterns in nature.

Responses

Unfortunately for later scholars, Hume did not frequently respond to the few philosophers who criticized his ideas. He dismissed one critic, the poet and philosopher James Beattie,* outright, calling him (in a letter to his publisher) a "bigoted silly fellow."

Hume did respond briefly, in private correspondence, to Reid, whose criticisms did not impress him. He accused Reid of believing in innate* ideas, ideas we are born with. This contrasted starkly with empiricism*—the belief that we derive our ideas from sense experience. The concept of innate ideas had become very unpopular, especially in Britain, so Hume's use of the phrase was the equivalent of calling Reid an old-fashioned thinker. Although, Hume may have misunderstood Reid's argument. Reid's point, at least in part, is that perception and thought relate to things outside of us. The objects of perception, for example, are not ideas but things in the world, such as orange balls.

Perhaps we can understand Hume's point by thinking again about causation. Reid said that things have causal powers, but he did not claim that we can perceive those causal powers. So how do our minds even grasp the concept of causation? If it does not come from perception, Hume thought, it must be innate.

In the nineteenth and early twentieth centuries, philosophers generally felt that Hume had won the argument. During the twentieth century, Reid came to be re-evaluated. Many philosophers today are sympathetic both with direct perception and the idea that causal powers are real. Today, it seems fair to say that some philosophers agree with Hume and others with Reid. After hundreds of years of debate, there has been no agreement on a single position.

Conflict And Consensus

The German philosopher Immanuel Kant,* another of Hume's contemporaries, claimed that when he read Hume's work, he was "awoken from his dogmatic slumber."[2] Kant found something profoundly disturbing in Hume's argument: He disagreed with it, but he recognized its power and felt it urgently required a response. Kant's later philosophy can be seen, to a large extent, as a response to Hume. For Kant, Hume had shown that we do not derive our knowledge of cause and effect from experience. Nevertheless, science shows that we do have such knowledge. So, Kant argued, our knowledge of cause and effect must be based not on experience but purely on reason. It would have been interesting to see how Hume reacted to this argument, but he died before Kant finally published his response, *Critique of Pure Reason*, in 1781.[3]

According to Kant, Hume's work highlighted a problem with the scientific method. Science tests very general conclusions by looking at particular instances. For example, we claim that all animals with hearts also have kidneys, and we test this hypothesis by checking every species that we can. But such testing can never be enough to establish the general conclusion, because we might discover a new species that has a heart but not a kidney—a complication called the problem of induction.* Hume was thought to have shown that inductive reasoning was inadequate to establish scientific conclusions. As a result, philosophers thought that to respond to Hume's arguments they had either to show that scientific method was not open to the problem of induction, or to accept that scientific knowledge is impossible.

NOTES

1   Thomas Reid, *An Inquiry into the Human Mind on the Principles of Common Sense* (University Park: Pennsylvania State University Press, 1997).

2   Immanuel Kant, *Prolegomena to Any Future Metaphysics*, trans. and ed. Gary Hatfield (Cambridge: Cambridge University Press, 1997), 10.

3   Immanuel Kant, *Critique of Pure Reason*, translated by Paul Guyer and Allen W. Wood (Cambridge: Cambridge University Press, 1997).

MODULE 10
THE EVOLVING DEBATE

KEY POINTS

- Hume's *Enquiry* spurred an enduring debate about the possibility of empirical knowledge and the validity of induction*, that is, testing general conclusions by looking at particular instances.

- Its arguments influenced philosophers such as the logical positivists* to dismiss metaphysics* as meaningless.

- Contemporary philosophical naturalists* have learned much from Hume.

Uses And Problems

Philosophers in the nineteenth and twentieth centuries reading *An Enquiry Concerning Human Understanding* and David Hume's other works believed that he had demonstrated the limits of empiricism.* Hume assumed that empiricism is true: all our beliefs about the world are based on sensory experience alone. He also showed how little could ultimately be proven by sensory experience. If empiricism is "correct," and we reason entirely empirically, we cannot reach any general truths about the world, or gain insight into the causal order of nature, let alone reach beyond the natural world to discover metaphysical truths about God or immortality. Hume's work also made the problem of induction a major challenge for epistemology*— the philosophical study of knowledge—and the philosophy of science.

Some theorists, among them, the nineteenth-century British philosopher and economist John Stuart Mill,* responded to Hume by outlining a scientific method which, they thought, would generate rationally believable but not entirely certain results if followed well.[1]

❝ When we run over libraries, persuaded of these principles, what havoc must we make? If we take in our hand any volume; of divinity or school metaphysics, for instance; let us ask, Does it contain any abstract reasoning concerning quantity or number? No. Does it contain any experimental reasoning concerning matter of fact and existence? No. Commit it then to the flames: For it can contain nothing but sophistry and illusion. ❞

David Hume, *An Enquiry Concerning Human Understanding*

The method of induction they advocated would be rational—distinguishing between good and bad science—but it would also necessarily be untrustworthy. One could never be certain that the good science is true. In the twentieth century, the philosopher Karl Popper* made a more radical proposal: that science does not need to use induction at all.[2] Popper noted that the general theories scientists put forward are merely guesses and are not based on evidence; scientific rigor comes into play only by devising experiments to test these guesses. In Popper's view, science consists only in *disproving* hypotheses (or assumptions) through experiment, not in *establishing* them.

Another tradition, one that began with the work of the German philosopher Immanuel Kant,* proposed a different response to Hume's ideas. Kant and his followers agreed that sensory experience alone could not establish knowledge about the world. Accordingly, they thought, we need certain *a priori** principles—that is, principles known independently of experience. Knowledge that the world is governed by causation, Kant thought, for example, is *a priori*.

But how can such *a priori* principles be justified? How can they be distinguished from irrational beliefs or mere prejudices? Although at this point questions become very complicated, Kant thought (in brief) that *a priori* principles could only be justified insofar as they applied to the realm of possible experience. We can be sure that everything we are capable of experiencing is governed by causation, but we cannot be sure that everything that exists is so governed.

Schools Of Thought

Kant's theory relates to another major evolutionary effect of Hume's thought. Hume taught many philosophers to be suspicious of metaphysics,* traditionally understood as the study of the fundamental nature of reality. However, Hume emphasizes the ways in which our knowledge of the world is limited by the sort of creatures we are. His work made many thinkers doubt that human beings were capable of acquiring metaphysical knowledge. Anti-metaphysical thinkers of the twentieth century, notably logical-positivist* philosophers such as Rudolf Carnap,* a leading philosopher in Vienna before World War II,* and his British contemporary A. J. Ayer,* were greatly influenced by Hume, either directly or through Kant.[3]

Indeed, logical-positivist philosophy can be seen as a radicalization of Hume's. Hume argues that only two things can improve our knowledge and understanding of the world: first, the kinds of empiricism found in the sciences, where observations and experiments are relied on; and second, mathematics. In Hume's view, disciplines such as metaphysics and theology,* which belong to neither category, do not add to knowledge. The logical positivists took this line of reasoning even further, saying that these other disciplines are not meaningful at all. As the logical positivists see it, metaphysicians and theologians not only fail to discover new truths about the world, they actually talk nonsense. Statements like "God made the world," if they cannot be tested by experiment and observations, have no meaning at all.

In Current Scholarship

Today's political scholars recognize Paine's *Common Sense* as a Hume's influence survived the decline of logical positivism's popularity in the middle of the twentieth century, a time when it became more common to interpret him as a philosophical naturalist.* Naturalists see philosophers and scientists as engaged in the same project of understanding the natural world. Naturalists have found inspiration in Hume's works, seeing their primary purpose as to create a science of the mind, and in this way to bring human beings more fully into the domain of science.

This project made sense to naturalistic philosophers such as the American academic W. V. Quine,* who argues in his article "Epistemology Naturalized"[4] that epistemology*—the philosophical study of knowledge—should be reconceived as part of psychology. Philosophers interested in knowledge should use scientific methods to study the ways in which knowledge is produced by human beings. This would involve studying the actual operations of the mind (how our perceptions give rise to beliefs, for example). Quine's naturalized epistemology is, as he acknowledges, very much in the spirit of Hume, and more recent philosophers such as Alvin Goldman* have advanced the theory.

More broadly, recent philosophy has moved toward seeing the human mind as part of nature, subject to the same laws as other natural objects and capable of being explained in the same way. This attitude is fundamentally Humean.

NOTES

1 John Stuart Mill, *A System of Logic* (London: John W. Parker, 1843).

2 Karl Popper, *Conjectures and Refutations* (London: Routledge, 2002), 60.

3 A. J. Ayer, *Language, Truth and Logic* (London: Gollancz, 1946); Ayer ed., *Logical Positivism* (New York: Free Press, 1959).

4 W.V. Quine, "Epistemology Naturalized" in *Ontological Relativity and Other Essays* (New York: Columbia, 1969).

MODULE 11
IMPACT AND INFLUENCE TODAY

KEY POINTS

- *Enquiry* is a classic exploration of the limits of empirical* knowledge.

- It challenges the ideas that experience can provide an adequate account of knowledge, and that we can have any real knowledge of necessary truths, except for those which are very trivial.

- Philosophers have responded by attempting to close Hume's gap between experience and theory.

Position

Many of the challenges to contemporary thought presented by David Hume's work, those of *An Enquiry Concerning Human Understanding* especially, come from his strict empiricism.* Empiricism claims that all our knowledge comes from experience. If, therefore, we have beliefs that go beyond what experience can teach us, we can only guess at them; these are things we cannot *know*. Empiricism can lead to certain sorts of skepticism* (that is, the denial that we can attain various forms of knowledge). While many philosophers have agreed with empiricism, few have applied it as consistently as Hume did.

If *Enquiry* has become a philosophical classic, it is partly because it is regarded as presenting a challenge that has yet to be answered. It challenges the idea that experience, as defined in the empiricist tradition, can provide an adequate foundation for our beliefs about the world. Philosophers respond to the challenge in different ways. Some, among them the twentieth century American philosopher W. V. Quine,* accept Hume's argument, and reject the project of providing

> ❝I do not see that we are farther along today than where Hume left us. The Humean predicament is the human predicament ❞
> W. V. Quine, "Epistemology Naturalized"

foundations for knowledge. Others, such as the South African philosopher John McDowell,* regard Hume as demonstrating that the empiricist conception of experience is inadequate. In their view, perceptual experience is richer than Hume thought. With a suitably wide conception of experience, they believe that experience can indeed provide a foundation for knowledge.

Interaction

Humeans tend towards skepticism* on the issue of causation.* Most of us naturally think of events *causing* each other, or of things having causal power. We see a ball hit a window and we see the window smash, so we think that the impact of the ball caused the smashing of the window. Humean skepticism doubts that we are entitled to this belief: all we have experienced is one event following another. We cannot attribute any causation to nature.

Humeans also argue that we cannot know any necessary truths (except perhaps very trivial ones). Hume distinguished between what he called "matters of fact"* and "relations of ideas."* In his view, all truths about the empirical world, the world of nature, are matters of fact. Relations of ideas pertain, rather, to our own concepts.

Mathematics offers relations of ideas: two plus two must always equal four; no other answer is possible. A non-mathematical example of a relation of ideas is the connection between being a bachelor and being unmarried. It is a necessary truth that all bachelors are unmarried; a married man would simply not count as being a bachelor. But Hume argues that such truths only tell us about the content of the concept "bachelor" and not about the real world.

This presents a challenge to philosophers who see themselves as investigating necessary truths about the world—the traditional concept behind metaphysics.* The special sciences, like physics or biology, discover truths about the world that are subject to chance; very general, necessary truths, on the other hand, are the realm of metaphysics.* Humeans doubt there are any such truths for metaphysics to study, or believe that if such truths do exist, we cannot gain any concrete knowledge of them.

The Continuing Debate

Hume denied that perceptual experience on its own is sufficient to yield knowledge about the world. Influenced by the German philosopher Immanuel Kant,* some thinkers respond that perception is richer and is capable of yielding more knowledge than Hume argued. A prominent contemporary promoter of this view is John McDowell, who argues in his book *Mind and World*[1] that perceptual experience is rich in concepts. In his view, the kind of perceptual experience human beings are capable of having depends on our conceptual abilities. Different people see dogs differently, for example, because of the background knowledge we possess about dogs.

Hume makes an important assumption that *empirical* truths—truths that can be discovered by observation and experiment—cannot be *necessary* truths,* because necessary truths are the kinds of things one cannot logically deny. Mathematical truths, for example, seem to be necessary: It is not only true that two plus two is four, but it could not be otherwise. Hume thought that mathematical truths can be arrived at *a priori*,* by using reason on its own, without reference to experience. The truths that we discover empirically can only be contingent; our beliefs about necessity in nature—for example, causal necessity—cannot be established as true by empirical research alone.

In one of the most important philosophical works of recent

decades, *Naming and Necessity*,[2] the American analytical philosopher Saul Kripke* argued against this Humean thesis. According to Kripke, some necessary truths can also be empirical; scientists have established this fact. For example, Kripke argues, it is a necessary truth that water is composed of hydrogen and oxygen—any substance that did not have this composition would not be water. But chemists had to do a great deal of empirical research to discover this truth. Kripke has played an important role in restoring metaphysics to a central place in philosophy.

In different ways, both McDowell and Kripke aim to close the Humean gap between experience and theory, helping to vindicate the idea that our beliefs—including our beliefs about causal processes and necessary truths—can sometimes be supported by experience.

NOTES

1   John McDowell, *Mind and World* (Cambridge, Mass.: Harvard University Press, 1996).

2   Saul Kripke, *Naming and Necessity* (Oxford: Blackwell, 1980).

MODULE 12
WHERE NEXT?

KEY POINTS

- The topics discussed in *Enquiry*, including the nature of causation and the nature of mind, remain controversial in philosophy and psychology.

- Some important contemporary thinkers continue to advance Humean solutions to these problems.

- *Enquiry* is a crucial text in the history of empiricism,* naturalism,* and skepticism.*

Potential

Over two hundred years after its publication, philosophers and psychologists still debate many of the arguments David Hume raises in *An Enquiry Concerning Human Understanding.* One such argument revolves around the nature of causation: Are causal laws simply patterns or regularities in nature? Or are causes, rather, real powers that explain why such patterns hold? Take, for example, the claim that smoking causes cancer. Does this mean merely that those who smoke are in fact more likely to contract cancer? Or does it mean there is something in the nature of smoking that brings about cancer?

A second subject for debate is the nature of the mind. Like other empiricists,* Hume believed that everything in the mind comes from experience. Much current discussion revolves around the issue of concepts (that is, the general categories in terms of which we understand the world). For example, when I sort the cutlery into knives, forks and spoons, I am employing three concepts to categorize the contents of the cutlery drawer. The question then arises: Where do my concepts come from? Do they all come from experience? Or are

> **❝** [Hume's] commanding presence in philosophy lies in the clarity of vision, the fact that time and time again he sees so exactly how things stand with us. **❞**
>
> Simon Blackburn, *How to Read Hume*

some or all of them derived from some other source such as my genetic inheritance, for example?

Future Directions

Many contemporary philosophers follow or echo various doctrines put forward by Hume. A smaller but still substantial number of philosophers have done work that has been so shaped by Hume that they might be called "Humeans."

One such thinker is the British philosopher Helen Beebee,* a scholar of Hume whose original philosophical work, especially in the field of metaphysics,* also shows his influence. Beebee defends a Humean conception of the laws of nature,* those very general laws of the universe which are discovered by science. According to her, these laws do not govern nature. They do not determine what will happen in the universe but, rather, merely describe very general natural patterns.[1] More broadly, Beebee argues that there is no necessity in nature: Everything in nature, including all that can be observed and investigated by natural science, is merely chance.

If Beebee defends a Humean metaphysics, the American philosopher Jesse Prinz* has argued for a Humean philosophy of mind. In his book *Furnishing the Mind*,[2] Prinz argues that we derive concepts from perceptual experience. This is empiricism,* a doctrine that has been frequently criticized since Hume's time. But Prinz offers a sophisticated defense of empiricism, drawing on modern psychology and cognitive science (the study of the mind and its processes). Hume's eighteenth-century world view is, Prinz thinks, largely supported by twenty-first-century science.

Summary

Without a doubt, David Hume's *An Enquiry Concerning Human Understanding* has earned its place as one of the great works of the western philosophical tradition. Despite being a short work, it has profoundly influenced philosophical discussion on a number of different topics and has given rise to several different streams of thought.

Some of the book's influence stems from the consistency and single-mindedness with which Hume pursues the consequences of empiricism.* Like other empiricists, he assumes that everything in the mind comes from the senses. But Hume drew consequences from this assumption that no previous empiricist had drawn. His *Enquiry* put the issue of causation, for example, at the center of philosophical discussion by raising profound doubts about whether causal powers in nature are open to observation. All we can observe, Hume said, are regular, repeated patterns in nature.

Ever since Hume, philosophers have wondered what causation is, and whether there is anything to the notion other than regularity in nature. Hume also cast profound doubts on conventional religious beliefs by questioning whether a belief in miracles could be justified on empiricist grounds.

If *Enquiry* is a pinnacle of the empiricist tradition, it is also a pioneering work in another philosophical tradition: naturalism.*

Hume undertook a scientific investigation of the human mind, applying to it the same principles that we use in the study of other parts of nature. Such an approach, if successful, would confirm the status of human beings as simply a part of the natural world, no different to non-human animals; humans have their own distinctive features, but they are not essentially distinct from the rest of nature. Naturalistic philosophers made great advances during the twentieth century and although much of contemporary naturalism would be unrecognizable to Hume, it is still very much in his spirit.

Enquiry is also a landmark in the modern discussion of skepticism,* a challenging epistemological issue* with which philosophers have struggled since the seventeenth century, when René Descartes wrote his major works.* Descartes debated with an imaginary skeptical opponent to show that it is, after all, possible to gain genuine knowledge of the world.

Although philosophers differ in their opinions of how successfully Descartes disproved the skeptical argument, Hume's discussion, raising the possibility that skepticism cannot be answered at an intellectual level, was different: how should we live, he asked, given that we cannot disprove the skeptic?

NOTES

1   Helen Beebee, "The Non-Governing Conception of Laws of Nature," *Philosophy and Phenomenological Research* 56 (2000): 571–594.

2   Jesse Prinz, *Furnishing the Mind: Concepts and their Perceptual Basis* (Cambridge: MIT Press, 2002).

GLOSSARY

GLOSSARY OF TERMS

a priori: *a priori* knowledge is knowledge held independently of experience.

Church of Scotland: the Protestant national church of Scotland.

Contingent truths: things that are true but are not required to be true. A "contingent truth" is the opposite of a "necessary truth". It is true that Berlin is the capital of Germany, for example—but is not a necessary truth, as the capital could just as easily be Bonn.

Empiricism: the view that all human knowledge comes from experience.

Epistemology: the philosophical study of knowledge.

Idealism: the view that there is no reality independent of our minds.

Ideas: in Hume's theory of the mind, ideas are copies of sense experience, held in the mind. We copy our idea of yellow, for example, from our visual experiences of yellow things.

Impressions: in Hume's theory of the mind, impressions are sense experiences. The other contents of the mind, ideas, are copies of impressions.

Induction: the process of assuming general principles from particular instances.

Innateness: innate characteristics are those with which human beings are born, as opposed to learned characteristics.

Logical positivism: a radical philosophical movement emphasizing the logical analysis of language. Logical positivists were active from the late 1920s, especially in Austria and Germany.

Matters of fact: matters concerning the way the world is. For Hume, these can only be known as a result of observation and experiment.

Metaphysics: an area of *philosophy* that looks to explain the nature of *being* and the *world* around it.

Miracle: a remarkable event attributed to divine or supernatural causes.

Naturalism: in philosophy, naturalism is the view that philosophy and science are engaged in the same project and use essentially the same methods.

Necessary truths: truths that, unlike contingent truths, could not have been otherwise. It is a necessary truth that bachelors are unmarried: no bachelor could possibly be married.

Phenomenology: the study of the ways in which the world appears to people.

Realism: the view that the world is independent of the mind.

Relations of ideas: for Hume, relations of ideas can, unlike matters of fact, be known with certainty independently of experience. They include the truths of mathematics.

Skepticism: the view that genuine knowledge of the world is impossible.

Scottish Enlightenment: the name given by historians to a fertile period of development in Scottish science, philosophy and literature during the eighteenth century.

Solipsism: the view that other people do not exist. Each solipsist believes that he or she is the only existing person.

Sophistry: the art of producing arguments that are superficially believable but not rationally convincing.

Testimony: the transmission of knowledge from one person to another, either through speech or through writing.

Theology: the study of God and religious belief.

World War II (1939–45): a global war between the vast majority of states, including all the great powers of the time.

PEOPLE MENTIONED IN THE TEXT

A. J. Ayer (1910–89) was an English philosopher best known for popularizing logical positivism in Britain and the United States.

Pierre Bayle (1647–1706) was a French philosopher and essayist, who emphasized the limitations of human reason and the impossibility of gaining certain knowledge.

James Beattie (1735–1803) was a Scottish poet and philosopher best known for his work in moral philosophy.

Helen Beebee is a British philosopher best known for her work on metaphysics and on Hume.

George Berkeley (1685–1753) was an Irish philosopher who argued for empiricism and idealism.

Simon Blackburn (b. 1944) is an English philosopher known for his attempts to popularize the discipline.

Robert Boyle (1627–91) was an Irish scientist, a founder of chemistry, and one of the most important scientists of his century.

Rudolf Carnap (1891–1970) was a German philosopher and leader of the logical-positivist movement. He contributed to logic, the philosophy of language and the philosophy of science.

Samuel Clarke (1675–1729) was an English philosopher and theologian who defended Isaac Newton's philosophical views and argued for the existence of God.

Gilles Deleuze (1925–95) was a French philosopher best known for his work in metaphysics and the philosophy of art.

René Descartes (1596–1650) was a French scientist, mathematician and philosopher who is regarded as one of the most important philosophers of the modern era.

Alvin Goldman (b. 1938) is an American philosopher best known for his work in epistemology.

Edmund Husserl (1859–1938) was a German philosopher considered to be the founder of phenomenology (the study of the structures of experience and consciousness).

Francis Hutcheson (1694–1746) was a Scottish philosopher best known for his moral philosophy and for his theory of the emotions.

James Hutton (1726–97) was a Scottish scientist who is regarded as the founder of modern geology.

Immanuel Kant (1724–1804) was a German philosopher who wrote *The Critique of Pure Reason* (1781). He is regarded as perhaps the most influential philosopher of the modern era.

Saul Kripke (b. 1940) is an American philosopher who has contributed to logic, philosophy of language, and numerous other fields and is widely regarded as one of the most important contemporary philosophers.

John Locke (1632–1704) was an English philosopher noted for his contributions to epistemology, philosophy of mind and political philosophy.

J. L. Mackie (1917–1981) was an Australian philosopher who contributed to ethics, metaphysics, and the philosophy of religion.

John McDowell (b. 1942) is a British philosopher who has written on topics as diverse as Aristotle, ethics, epistemology, and the philosophy of mind.

John Stuart Mill (1806–73) was an English philosopher, known for his contributions to philosophy of science and to ethics and political philosophy.

Isaac Newton (1642–1727) was an English scientist, mathematician and philosopher. He is frequently regarded as one of the greatest physicists and mathematicians who ever lived.

Karl Popper (1902–94) was an Austrian philosopher. He is perhaps one of the best-known philosophers of science of the twentieth century.

Jesse Prinz is an American philosopher and cognitive scientist who has written both for academic and popular audiences on psychology, the emotions and aesthetics.

Pyrrho of Elis (c. 360–270 B.C.E.) was an ancient Greek philosopher. Although he did not write anything, he is thought to have been a radical skeptic who believed that knowledge is impossible and that human beings should not attempt to know anything about the world.

W.V. Quine (1908–2000) was an American philosopher who contributed to logic, philosophy of language, epistemology, and the philosophy of science.

Thomas Reid (1710–69) was a Scottish philosopher who is best known today for his theory of perception.

Sextus Empiricus (c. 160–210) was a Greek physician best known for his writings on epistemology, in which he showed he was in favor of a form of skepticism.

Adam Smith (1723–90) was a Scottish philosopher and economist, regarded as one of the founders of modern economics.

James St Clair (1688–1762) was a Scottish soldier and politician.

Galen Strawson (b. 1952) is a British philosopher who has written on metaphysics, the philosophy of mind, and the history of philosophy.

James Watt (1736–1819) was a Scottish engineer who invented the modern steam engine.

WORKS CITED

WORKS CITED

Ayer, A. J. *Language, Truth and Logic*. London: Gollancz, 1946.

ed., *Logical Positivism*. New York: Free Press, 1959.

Beebee, Helen. "The Non-Governing Conception of Laws of Nature." *Philosophy and Phenomenological Research* 56 (2000): 571–594.

Deleuze, Gilles. *Empiricism and Subjectivity*. Translated by Constantin V. Boundas. New York: Columbia University Press, 1991.

Hume, David. *A Treatise of Human Nature*. Oxford: Oxford University Press, 1978.

Essays Moral, Political and Literary. Indianopolis: Liberty Classics, 1985.

"My Own Life." In *The Cambridge Companion to Hume*. Edited by David Fate Norton. Cambridge: Cambridge University Press, 1993.

An Enquiry Concerning Human Understanding. Cambridge: Cambridge University *Dialogues Concerning Natural Religion*. Cambridge: Cambridge University Press, 2007.

Husserl, Edmund. *The Crisis of the European Sciences and Transcendental Phenomenology.* Translated by David Carr. Evanston: Northwestern University Press.

Kant, Immanuel. *Critique of Pure Reason*. Translated by Paul Guyer and Allen W. Wood. Cambridge: Cambridge University Press, 1997.

Prolegomena to Any Future Metaphysics. Translated and edited by Gary Hatfield. Cambridge: Cambridge University Press, 1997.

Kripke, Saul. *Naming and Necessity*. Oxford: Blackwell, 1980.

Lackey, Jennifer and Ernest Sosa, eds. *The Epistemology of Testimony*. Oxford: Oxford University Press, 2006.

Mackie, J. L. *The Miracle of Theism: Arguments For and Against the Existence of God*. Oxford: Oxford University Press, 1982.

McDowell, John. *Mind and World*. Cambridge, Mass.: Harvard University Press, 1996.

Mill, John Stuart. *A System of Logic*. London: John W. Parker, 1843.

Moore, James. "Hutcheson and Hume." In *Hume and Hume's Connexions*. Edited by M. A. Stewart and John P. Wright. Edinburgh: Edinburgh University Press, 1990.

Popper, Karl. *Conjectures and Refutations*. London: Routledge, 2002.

Prinz, Jesse. *Furnishing the Mind: Concepts and their Perceptual Basis*. Cambridge: MIT Press, 2002.

Quine, W.V. "Epistemology Naturalized." In *Ontological Relativity and Other Essays*. New York: Columbia University Press, 1969.

Reid, Thomas. *An Enquiry into the Human Mind on the Principles of Common Sense*. University Park, PA: Pennsylvania State University Press, 1997.

Smith, Norman Kemp. *The Philosophy of David Hume*. London: Macmillan, 1941.

Strawson, Galen. *The Secret Connexion: Causation, Realism and David Hume*. Oxford: Clarendon Press, 1989.

Weis, Charles and Frederick Pottle. *Boswell in Extremes, 1776-1778*. New York: McGraw-Hill, 1970.

THE MACAT LIBRARY
BY DISCIPLINE

AFRICANA STUDIES

Chinua Achebe's *An Image of Africa: Racism in Conrad's Heart of Darkness*
W. E. B. Du Bois's *The Souls of Black Folk*
Zora Neale Huston's *Characteristics of Negro Expression*
Martin Luther King Jr's *Why We Can't Wait*
Toni Morrison's *Playing in the Dark: Whiteness in the American Literary Imagination*

ANTHROPOLOGY

Arjun Appadurai's *Modernity at Large: Cultural Dimensions of Globalisation*
Philippe Ariès's *Centuries of Childhood*
Franz Boas's *Race, Language and Culture*
Kim Chan & Renée Mauborgne's *Blue Ocean Strategy*
Jared Diamond's *Guns, Germs & Steel: the Fate of Human Societies*
Jared Diamond's *Collapse: How Societies Choose to Fail or Survive*
E. E. Evans-Pritchard's *Witchcraft, Oracles and Magic Among the Azande*
James Ferguson's *The Anti-Politics Machine*
Clifford Geertz's *The Interpretation of Cultures*
David Graeber's *Debt: the First 5000 Years*
Karen Ho's *Liquidated: An Ethnography of Wall Street*
Geert Hofstede's *Culture's Consequences: Comparing Values, Behaviors, Institutes and Organizations across Nations*
Claude Lévi-Strauss's *Structural Anthropology*
Jay Macleod's *Ain't No Makin' It: Aspirations and Attainment in a Low-Income Neighborhood*
Saba Mahmood's *The Politics of Piety: The Islamic Revival and the Feminist Subject*
Marcel Mauss's *The Gift*

BUSINESS

Jean Lave & Etienne Wenger's *Situated Learning*
Theodore Levitt's *Marketing Myopia*
Burton G. Malkiel's *A Random Walk Down Wall Street*
Douglas McGregor's *The Human Side of Enterprise*
Michael Porter's *Competitive Strategy: Creating and Sustaining Superior Performance*
John Kotter's *Leading Change*
C. K. Prahalad & Gary Hamel's *The Core Competence of the Corporation*

CRIMINOLOGY

Michelle Alexander's *The New Jim Crow: Mass Incarceration in the Age of Colorblindness*
Michael R. Gottfredson & Travis Hirschi's *A General Theory of Crime*
Richard Herrnstein & Charles A. Murray's *The Bell Curve: Intelligence and Class Structure in American Life*
Elizabeth Loftus's *Eyewitness Testimony*
Jay Macleod's *Ain't No Makin' It: Aspirations and Attainment in a Low-Income Neighborhood*
Philip Zimbardo's *The Lucifer Effect*

ECONOMICS

Janet Abu-Lughod's *Before European Hegemony*
Ha-Joon Chang's *Kicking Away the Ladder*
David Brion Davis's *The Problem of Slavery in the Age of Revolution*
Milton Friedman's *The Role of Monetary Policy*
Milton Friedman's *Capitalism and Freedom*
David Graeber's *Debt: the First 5000 Years*
Friedrich Hayek's *The Road to Serfdom*
Karen Ho's *Liquidated: An Ethnography of Wall Street*

John Maynard Keynes's *The General Theory of Employment, Interest and Money*
Charles P. Kindleberger's *Manias, Panics and Crashes*
Robert Lucas's *Why Doesn't Capital Flow from Rich to Poor Countries?*
Burton G. Malkiel's *A Random Walk Down Wall Street*
Thomas Robert Malthus's *An Essay on the Principle of Population*
Karl Marx's *Capital*
Thomas Piketty's *Capital in the Twenty-First Century*
Amartya Sen's *Development as Freedom*
Adam Smith's *The Wealth of Nations*
Nassim Nicholas Taleb's *The Black Swan: The Impact of the Highly Improbable*
Amos Tversky's & Daniel Kahneman's *Judgment under Uncertainty: Heuristics and Biases*
Mahbub Ul Haq's *Reflections on Human Development*
Max Weber's *The Protestant Ethic and the Spirit of Capitalism*

FEMINISM AND GENDER STUDIES

Judith Butler's *Gender Trouble*
Simone De Beauvoir's *The Second Sex*
Michel Foucault's *History of Sexuality*
Betty Friedan's *The Feminine Mystique*
Saba Mahmood's *The Politics of Piety: The Islamic Revival and the Feminist Subject*
Joan Wallach Scott's *Gender and the Politics of History*
Mary Wollstonecraft's *A Vindication of the Rights of Woman*
Virginia Woolf's *A Room of One's Own*

GEOGRAPHY

The Brundtland Report's *Our Common Future*
Rachel Carson's *Silent Spring*
Charles Darwin's *On the Origin of Species*
James Ferguson's *The Anti-Politics Machine*
Jane Jacobs's *The Death and Life of Great American Cities*
James Lovelock's *Gaia: A New Look at Life on Earth*
Amartya Sen's *Development as Freedom*
Mathis Wackernagel & William Rees's *Our Ecological Footprint*

HISTORY

Janet Abu-Lughod's *Before European Hegemony*
Benedict Anderson's *Imagined Communities*
Bernard Bailyn's *The Ideological Origins of the American Revolution*
Hanna Batatu's *The Old Social Classes And The Revolutionary Movements Of Iraq*
Christopher Browning's *Ordinary Men: Reserve Police Batallion 101 and the Final Solution in Poland*
Edmund Burke's *Reflections on the Revolution in France*
William Cronon's *Nature's Metropolis: Chicago And The Great West*
Alfred W. Crosby's *The Columbian Exchange*
Hamid Dabashi's *Iran: A People Interrupted*
David Brion Davis's *The Problem of Slavery in the Age of Revolution*
Nathalie Zemon Davis's *The Return of Martin Guerre*
Jared Diamond's *Guns, Germs & Steel: the Fate of Human Societies*
Frank Dikotter's *Mao's Great Famine*
John W Dower's *War Without Mercy: Race And Power In The Pacific War*
W. E. B. Du Bois's *The Souls of Black Folk*
Richard J. Evans's *In Defence of History*
Lucien Febvre's *The Problem of Unbelief in the 16th Century*
Sheila Fitzpatrick's *Everyday Stalinism*

The Macat Library By Discipline

LITERATURE

Chinua Achebe's *An Image of Africa: Racism in Conrad's Heart of Darkness*
Roland Barthes's *Mythologies*
Homi K. Bhabha's *The Location of Culture*
Judith Butler's *Gender Trouble*
Simone De Beauvoir's *The Second Sex*
Ferdinand De Saussure's *Course in General Linguistics*
T. S. Eliot's *The Sacred Wood: Essays on Poetry and Criticism*
Zora Neale Huston's *Characteristics of Negro Expression*
Toni Morrison's *Playing in the Dark: Whiteness in the American Literary Imagination*
Edward Said's *Orientalism*
Gayatri Chakravorty Spivak's *Can the Subaltern Speak?*
Mary Wollstonecraft's *A Vindication of the Rights of Women*
Virginia Woolf's *A Room of One's Own*

PHILOSOPHY

Elizabeth Anscombe's *Modern Moral Philosophy*
Hannah Arendt's *The Human Condition*
Aristotle's *Metaphysics*
Aristotle's *Nicomachean Ethics*
Edmund Gettier's *Is Justified True Belief Knowledge?*
Georg Wilhelm Friedrich Hegel's *Phenomenology of Spirit*
David Hume's *Dialogues Concerning Natural Religion*
David Hume's *The Enquiry for Human Understanding*
Immanuel Kant's *Religion within the Boundaries of Mere Reason*
Immanuel Kant's *Critique of Pure Reason*
Søren Kierkegaard's *The Sickness Unto Death*
Søren Kierkegaard's *Fear and Trembling*
C. S. Lewis's *The Abolition of Man*
Alasdair MacIntyre's *After Virtue*
Marcus Aurelius's *Meditations*
Friedrich Nietzsche's *On the Genealogy of Morality*
Friedrich Nietzsche's *Beyond Good and Evil*
Plato's *Republic*
Plato's *Symposium*
Jean-Jacques Rousseau's *The Social Contract*
Gilbert Ryle's *The Concept of Mind*
Baruch Spinoza's *Ethics*
Sun Tzu's *The Art of War*
Ludwig Wittgenstein's *Philosophical Investigations*

POLITICS

Benedict Anderson's *Imagined Communities*
Aristotle's *Politics*
Bernard Bailyn's *The Ideological Origins of the American Revolution*
Edmund Burke's *Reflections on the Revolution in France*
John C. Calhoun's *A Disquisition on Government*
Ha-Joon Chang's *Kicking Away the Ladder*
Hamid Dabashi's *Iran: A People Interrupted*
Hamid Dabashi's *Theology of Discontent: The Ideological Foundation of the Islamic Revolution in Iran*
Robert Dahl's *Democracy and its Critics*
Robert Dahl's *Who Governs?*
David Brion Davis's *The Problem of Slavery in the Age of Revolution*

The Macat Library By Discipline

Alexis De Tocqueville's *Democracy in America*
James Ferguson's *The Anti-Politics Machine*
Frank Dikotter's *Mao's Great Famine*
Sheila Fitzpatrick's *Everyday Stalinism*
Eric Foner's *Reconstruction: America's Unfinished Revolution, 1863-1877*
Milton Friedman's *Capitalism and Freedom*
Francis Fukuyama's *The End of History and the Last Man*
John Lewis Gaddis's *We Now Know: Rethinking Cold War History*
Ernest Gellner's *Nations and Nationalism*
David Graeber's *Debt: the First 5000 Years*
Antonio Gramsci's *The Prison Notebooks*
Alexander Hamilton, John Jay & James Madison's *The Federalist Papers*
Friedrich Hayek's *The Road to Serfdom*
Christopher Hill's *The World Turned Upside Down*
Thomas Hobbes's *Leviathan*
John A. Hobson's *Imperialism: A Study*
Samuel P. Huntington's *The Clash of Civilizations and the Remaking of World Order*
Tony Judt's *Postwar: A History of Europe Since 1945*
David C. Kang's *China Rising: Peace, Power and Order in East Asia*
Paul Kennedy's *The Rise and Fall of Great Powers*
Robert Keohane's *After Hegemony*
Martin Luther King Jr.'s *Why We Can't Wait*
Henry Kissinger's *World Order: Reflections on the Character of Nations and the Course of History*
John Locke's *Two Treatises of Government*
Niccolò Machiavelli's *The Prince*
Thomas Robert Malthus's *An Essay on the Principle of Population*
Mahmood Mamdani's *Citizen and Subject: Contemporary Africa And The Legacy Of Late Colonialism*
Karl Marx's *Capital*
John Stuart Mill's *On Liberty*
John Stuart Mill's *Utilitarianism*
Hans Morgenthau's *Politics Among Nations*
Thomas Paine's *Common Sense*
Thomas Paine's *Rights of Man*
Thomas Piketty's *Capital in the Twenty-First Century*
Robert D. Putman's *Bowling Alone*
John Rawls's *Theory of Justice*
Jean-Jacques Rousseau's *The Social Contract*
Theda Skocpol's *States and Social Revolutions*
Adam Smith's *The Wealth of Nations*
Sun Tzu's *The Art of War*
Henry David Thoreau's *Civil Disobedience*
Thucydides's *The History of the Peloponnesian War*
Kenneth Waltz's *Theory of International Politics*
Max Weber's *Politics as a Vocation*
Odd Arne Westad's *The Global Cold War: Third World Interventions And The Making Of Our Times*

POSTCOLONIAL STUDIES

Roland Barthes's *Mythologies*
Frantz Fanon's *Black Skin, White Masks*
Homi K. Bhabha's *The Location of Culture*
Gustavo Gutiérrez's *A Theology of Liberation*
Edward Said's *Orientalism*
Gayatri Chakravorty Spivak's *Can the Subaltern Speak?*

PSYCHOLOGY

Gordon Allport's *The Nature of Prejudice*
Alan Baddeley & Graham Hitch's *Aggression: A Social Learning Analysis*
Albert Bandura's *Aggression: A Social Learning Analysis*
Leon Festinger's *A Theory of Cognitive Dissonance*
Sigmund Freud's *The Interpretation of Dreams*
Betty Friedan's *The Feminine Mystique*
Michael R. Gottfredson & Travis Hirschi's *A General Theory of Crime*
Eric Hoffer's *The True Believer: Thoughts on the Nature of Mass Movements*
William James's *Principles of Psychology*
Elizabeth Loftus's *Eyewitness Testimony*
A. H. Maslow's *A Theory of Human Motivation*
Stanley Milgram's *Obedience to Authority*
Steven Pinker's *The Better Angels of Our Nature*
Oliver Sacks's *The Man Who Mistook His Wife For a Hat*
Richard Thaler & Cass Sunstein's *Nudge: Improving Decisions About Health, Wealth and Happiness*
Amos Tversky's *Judgment under Uncertainty: Heuristics and Biases*
Philip Zimbardo's *The Lucifer Effect*

SCIENCE

Rachel Carson's *Silent Spring*
William Cronon's *Nature's Metropolis: Chicago And The Great West*
Alfred W. Crosby's *The Columbian Exchange*
Charles Darwin's *On the Origin of Species*
Richard Dawkin's *The Selfish Gene*
Thomas Kuhn's *The Structure of Scientific Revolutions*
Geoffrey Parker's *Global Crisis: War, Climate Change and Catastrophe in the Seventeenth Century*
Mathis Wackernagel & William Rees's *Our Ecological Footprint*

SOCIOLOGY

Michelle Alexander's *The New Jim Crow: Mass Incarceration in the Age of Colorblindness*
Gordon Allport's *The Nature of Prejudice*
Albert Bandura's *Aggression: A Social Learning Analysis*
Hanna Batatu's *The Old Social Classes And The Revolutionary Movements Of Iraq*
Ha-Joon Chang's *Kicking Away the Ladder*
W. E. B. Du Bois's *The Souls of Black Folk*
Émile Durkheim's *On Suicide*
Frantz Fanon's *Black Skin, White Masks*
Frantz Fanon's *The Wretched of the Earth*
Eric Foner's *Reconstruction: America's Unfinished Revolution, 1863-1877*
Eugene Genovese's *Roll, Jordan, Roll: The World the Slaves Made*
Jack Goldstone's *Revolution and Rebellion in the Early Modern World*
Antonio Gramsci's *The Prison Notebooks*
Richard Herrnstein & Charles A Murray's *The Bell Curve: Intelligence and Class Structure in American Life*
Eric Hoffer's *The True Believer: Thoughts on the Nature of Mass Movements*
Jane Jacobs's *The Death and Life of Great American Cities*
Robert Lucas's *Why Doesn't Capital Flow from Rich to Poor Countries?*
Jay Macleod's *Ain't No Makin' It: Aspirations and Attainment in a Low Income Neighborhood*
Elaine May's *Homeward Bound: American Families in the Cold War Era*
Douglas McGregor's *The Human Side of Enterprise*
C. Wright Mills's *The Sociological Imagination*

Thomas Piketty's *Capital in the Twenty-First Century*
Robert D. Putman's *Bowling Alone*
David Riesman's *The Lonely Crowd: A Study of the Changing American Character*
Edward Said's *Orientalism*
Joan Wallach Scott's *Gender and the Politics of History*
Theda Skocpol's *States and Social Revolutions*
Max Weber's *The Protestant Ethic and the Spirit of Capitalism*

THEOLOGY

Augustine's *Confessions*
Benedict's *Rule of St Benedict*
Gustavo Gutiérrez's *A Theology of Liberation*
Carole Hillenbrand's *The Crusades: Islamic Perspectives*
David Hume's *Dialogues Concerning Natural Religion*
Immanuel Kant's *Religion within the Boundaries of Mere Reason*
Ernst Kantorowicz's *The King's Two Bodies: A Study in Medieval Political Theology*
Søren Kierkegaard's *The Sickness Unto Death*
C. S. Lewis's *The Abolition of Man*
Saba Mahmood's *The Politics of Piety: The Islamic Revival and the Feminist Subject*
Baruch Spinoza's *Ethics*
Keith Thomas's *Religion and the Decline of Magic*

COMING SOON

Chris Argyris's *The Individual and the Organisation*
Seyla Benhabib's *The Rights of Others*
Walter Benjamin's *The Work Of Art in the Age of Mechanical Reproduction*
John Berger's *Ways of Seeing*
Pierre Bourdieu's *Outline of a Theory of Practice*
Mary Douglas's *Purity and Danger*
Roland Dworkin's *Taking Rights Seriously*
James G. March's *Exploration and Exploitation in Organisational Learning*
Ikujiro Nonaka's *A Dynamic Theory of Organizational Knowledge Creation*
Griselda Pollock's *Vision and Difference*
Amartya Sen's *Inequality Re-Examined*
Susan Sontag's *On Photography*
Yasser Tabbaa's *The Transformation of Islamic Art*
Ludwig von Mises's *Theory of Money and Credit*

Macat Disciplines

Access the greatest ideas and thinkers across entire disciplines, including

AFRICANA STUDIES

Chinua Achebe's *An Image of Africa: Racism in Conrad's Heart of Darkness*

W. E. B. Du Bois's *The Souls of Black Folk*

Zora Neale Hurston's *Characteristics of Negro Expression*

Martin Luther King Jr.'s *Why We Can't Wait*

Toni Morrison's *Playing in the Dark: Whiteness in the American Literary Imagination*

Macat Disciplines

Access the greatest ideas and thinkers across entire disciplines, including

FEMINISM, GENDER AND QUEER STUDIES

Simone De Beauvoir's
The Second Sex

Michel Foucault's
History of Sexuality

Betty Friedan's
The Feminine Mystique

Saba Mahmood's
*The Politics of Piety:
The Islamic Revival and
the Feminist Subject*

Joan Wallach Scott's
*Gender and the
Politics of History*

Mary Wollstonecraft's
*A Vindication of the
Rights of Woman*

Virginia Woolf's
A Room of One's Own

Judith Butler's
Gender Trouble

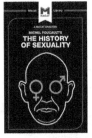

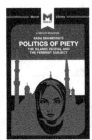

Macat analyses are available from all good bookshops and libraries.

Access hundreds of analyses through one, multimedia tool.
Join free for one month **library.macat.com**

Macat Disciplines

Access the greatest ideas and thinkers
across entire disciplines, including

INEQUALITY

Ha-Joon Chang's, *Kicking Away the Ladder*
David Graeber's, *Debt: The First 5000 Years*
Robert E. Lucas's, *Why Doesn't Capital Flow from Rich To Poor Countries?*
Thomas Piketty's, *Capital in the Twenty-First Century*
Amartya Sen's, *Inequality Re-Examined*
Mahbub Ul Haq's, *Reflections on Human Development*

Macat analyses are available from all good bookshops and libraries.

Access hundreds of analyses through one, multimedia tool.
Join free for one month **library.macat.com**

Macat Disciplines

Access the greatest ideas and thinkers across entire disciplines, including

CRIMINOLOGY

Michelle Alexander's
The New Jim Crow: Mass Incarceration in the Age of Colorblindness

Michael R. Gottfredson & Travis Hirschi's
A General Theory of Crime

Elizabeth Loftus's
Eyewitness Testimony

Richard Herrnstein & Charles A. Murray's
The Bell Curve: Intelligence and Class Structure in American Life

Jay Macleod's
Ain't No Makin' It: Aspirations and Attainment in a Low-Income Neighborhood

Philip Zimbardo's
The Lucifer Effect

Macat Disciplines

Access the greatest ideas and thinkers across entire disciplines, including

Postcolonial Studies

Roland Barthes's *Mythologies*
Frantz Fanon's *Black Skin, White Masks*
Homi K. Bhabha's *The Location of Culture*
Gustavo Gutiérrez's *A Theology of Liberation*
Edward Said's *Orientalism*
Gayatri Chakravorty Spivak's *Can the Subaltern Speak?*

Macat Disciplines

Access the greatest ideas and thinkers across entire disciplines, including

GLOBALIZATION

Arjun Appadurai's, *Modernity at Large: Cultural Dimensions of Globalisation*

James Ferguson's, *The Anti-Politics Machine*

Geert Hofstede's, *Culture's Consequences*

Amartya Sen's, *Development as Freedom*

Macat Pairs

*Analyse historical and modern issues
from opposite sides of an argument.
Pairs include:*

HOW TO RUN AN ECONOMY

John Maynard Keynes's
*The General Theory OF Employment,
Interest and Money*

Classical economics suggests that market economies
are self-correcting in times of recession or depression,
and tend toward full employment and output. But
English economist John Maynard Keynes disagrees.

In his ground-breaking 1936 study *The General
Theory*, Keynes argues that traditional economics
has misunderstood the causes of unemployment.
Employment is not determined by the price of labor;
it is directly linked to demand. Keynes believes market
economies are by nature unstable, and so require
government intervention. Spurred on by the social
catastrophe of the Great Depression of the 1930s,
he sets out to revolutionize the way the world thinks

Milton Friedman's
The Role of Monetary Policy

Friedman's 1968 paper changed the course of
economic theory. In just 17 pages, he demolished
existing theory and outlined an effective alternate
monetary policy designed to secure 'high employment,
stable prices and rapid growth.'

Friedman demonstrated that monetary policy plays
a vital role in broader economic stability and argued
that economists got their monetary policy wrong
in the 1950s and 1960s by misunderstanding the
relationship between inflation and unemployment.
Previous generations of economists had believed
that governments could permanently decrease
unemployment by permitting inflation—and vice versa.
Friedman's most original contribution was to show that
this supposed trade-off is an illusion that only works in
the short term.

Macat Disciplines

Access the greatest ideas and thinkers across entire disciplines, including

THE FUTURE OF DEMOCRACY

Robert A. Dahl's, *Democracy and Its Critics*
Robert A. Dahl's, *Who Governs?*
Alexis De Toqueville's, *Democracy in America*
Niccolò Machiavelli's, *The Prince*
John Stuart Mill's, *On Liberty*
Robert D. Putnam's, *Bowling Alone*
Jean-Jacques Rousseau's, *The Social Contract*
Henry David Thoreau's, *Civil Disobedience*

Macat Disciplines

Access the greatest ideas and thinkers across entire disciplines, including

TOTALITARIANISM

Sheila Fitzpatrick's, *Everyday Stalinism*
Ian Kershaw's, *The "Hitler Myth"*
Timothy Snyder's, *Bloodlands*

Macat Pairs

Analyse historical and modern issues from opposite sides of an argument. Pairs include:

RACE AND IDENTITY

Zora Neale Hurston's
Characteristics of Negro Expression

Using material collected on anthropological expeditions to the South, Zora Neale Hurston explains how expression in African American culture in the early twentieth century departs from the art of white America. At the time, African American art was often criticized for copying white culture. For Hurston, this criticism misunderstood how art works. European tradition views art as something fixed. But Hurston describes a creative process that is alive, ever-changing, and largely improvisational. She maintains that African American art works through a process called 'mimicry'—where an imitated object or verbal pattern, for example, is reshaped and altered until it becomes something new, novel—and worthy of attention.

Frantz Fanon's
Black Skin, White Masks

Black Skin, White Masks offers a radical analysis of the psychological effects of colonization on the colonized.

Fanon witnessed the effects of colonization first hand both in his birthplace, Martinique, and again later in life when he worked as a psychiatrist in another French colony, Algeria. His text is uncompromising in form and argument. He dissects the dehumanizing effects of colonialism, arguing that it destroys the native sense of identity, forcing people to adapt to an alien set of values—including a core belief that they are inferior. This results in deep psychological trauma.

Fanon's work played a pivotal role in the civil rights movements of the 1960s.

Macat analyses are available from all good bookshops and libraries.

Access hundreds of analyses through one, multimedia tool.
Join free for one month **library.macat.com**

Macat Pairs

Analyse historical and modern issues from opposite sides of an argument. Pairs include:

INTERNATIONAL RELATIONS IN THE 21ST CENTURY

Samuel P. Huntington's
The Clash of Civilisations

In his highly influential 1996 book, Huntington offers a vision of a post-Cold War world in which conflict takes place not between competing ideologies but between cultures. The worst clash, he argues, will be between the Islamic world and the West: the West's arrogance and belief that its culture is a "gift" to the world will come into conflict with Islam's obstinacy and concern that its culture is under attack from a morally decadent "other."

Clash inspired much debate between different political schools of thought. But its greatest impact came in helping define American foreign policy in the wake of the 2001 terrorist attacks in New York and Washington.

Francis Fukuyama's
The End of History and the Last Man

Published in 1992, *The End of History and the Last Man* argues that capitalist democracy is the final destination for all societies. Fukuyama believed democracy triumphed during the Cold War because it lacks the "fundamental contradictions" inherent in communism and satisfies our yearning for freedom and equality. Democracy therefore marks the endpoint in the evolution of ideology, and so the "end of history." There will still be "events," but no fundamental change in ideology.

For Product Safety Concerns and Information please contact our EU
representative GPSR@taylorandfrancis.com Taylor & Francis Verlag GmbH,
Kaufingerstraße 24, 80331 München, Germany

Printed and bound by CPI Group (UK) Ltd, Croydon, CR0 4YY
08/06/2025
01896977-0001